DATE DUE

*Free Reserves
and the Money Supply*

This volume is a publication of the
Workshop in Money and Banking

*

STUDIES IN ECONOMICS

of the

ECONOMICS RESEARCH CENTER

of the

UNIVERSITY OF CHICAGO

Free Reserves
and the Money Supply

By
A. JAMES MEIGS

THE UNIVERSITY OF CHICAGO PRESS

Library of Congress Catalog Card Number: 62-17136

THE UNIVERSITY OF CHICAGO PRESS, CHICAGO & LONDON
The University of Toronto Press, Toronto 5, Canada

Foreword

A FASCINATING aspect of scientific research is the unexpected connections that are always turning up. Work on one problem turns out to have implications for a very different problem; the purest of theories has unexpected practical applications; and the most practical activities turn out to enrich pure theory.

This monograph is an excellent example. It deals with a highly special and technical problem in applied central banking: the connection between the actions of the Federal Reserve System and the behavior of the stock of money, with special reference to the role played by a particular intermediate magnitude, free reserves. This topic does not seem intimately connected with the pure theory of capital, a technical and difficult area in abstract economic theory which seeks to analyze the relations among the stock of capital, the flow of savings and investment, and the rate, or rates, of interest connecting them. If there be any connection, it would offhand seem to be that interest rates enter into both topics.

Yet some key ideas that have recently been developed in capital theory turned out to be of critical importance to Meigs in analyzing his central-banking problem; and, reciprocally, his work seems to me an important contribution to a wide range of capital theory problems having nothing to do with banking. Moreover, the ideas that were important for Meigs were only accidentally connected with interest rates. They had to do with the relation between stocks and flows, with the idea that the stock demanded at various prices (which may but need not be interest rates) itself depends on the rate at which the stock is being increased or decreased and, conversely, that the rate at which it is desired to increase or decrease the stock depends on the level of the stock. These notions in turn imply a distinction between full equilibrium positions and temporary equilibrium positions.

To put these ideas in another way, they involve distinguishing between two problems: (1) what determines the stock of assets the community desires to hold; (2) what determines the rate at which the community seeks to eliminate any discrepancy between its actual and its desired stock, or at which it goes from a stock desired under one set of circumstances to a stock desired under another? To illustrate with a homely example: suppose an earthquake wipes out half the housing in a

v

particular city. The factors that determine the new stock of housing that will be desired once reconstruction is complete are one thing; the factors that determine the rate at which reconstruction will proceed are another; yet the two are connected by the fact that at every point in time the existing stock is that which is demanded *given* that reconstruction is proceeding at the rate it is. The prices which produce this adjustment are in this example the sales price of houses, the costs involved in producing new houses, and the current and expected rental values of housing services.

Meigs's study is one of very few in which these ideas have been given empirical content and have been used to organize an empirical study. The ideas have contributed to his ability to make an important advance in the understanding of a central-banking problem of long standing; in turn, he has contributed notably to the theoretical ideas themselves, both by pushing the theory one step further than, so far as I know, it has been carried explicitly hitherto and by showing how it can be given empirical content.

The connection between these ideas and Meigs's problem is that a bank has a balance sheet of assets and liabilities—a "stock" concept—that is subject to change from moment to moment by current transactions—the "flows." The flows are the means whereby banks can and do deliberately alter their balance sheet; also, the flows may introduce unintended changes in the balance sheet that lead banks to set in train further flows.

The particular balance sheet items Meigs concentrates on are reserve balances in excess of required reserves and borrowings from the Federal Reserve. The difference is free reserves, a magnitude to which that large class of specialists scrutinizing the day-to-day activities of the Reserve System have come to attach almost mystical significance. The ratio of the difference to deposits is the free-reserve ratio. Suppose available reserves are constant but something happens to change the free-reserve ratio banks desire to maintain. They will then seek to move from the actual to the desired ratio by buying or selling assets and thereby producing a change in the free-reserve ratio. The absence of such purchases or sales means stability in the reserve ratio, which is then a sign that the actual and desired ratios are equal. So far, Meigs's analysis parallels the capital theory analysis.

Empirical study along these lines, however, led him to introduce another level of complexity, and this is where his analysis goes beyond the capital theory analysis. Suppose instead that the Federal Reserve starts changing the volume of reserves available. If banks do nothing, this will introduce a discrepancy between their actual and desired ratios. Hence they will do something. Stability in the actual reserve ratio may then mean not that banks are engaging in no purchases or sales intended to alter the desired ratio but that their actions are offsetting the Reserve System's actions. The free-reserve ratio is remaining stable because the banks, by their actions, produce a rate of change in deposits just large enough to absorb or release the change in reserves available. The ratio is then in what Meigs calls a position of secondary equilibrium.

This sophisticated theoretical apparatus, which Meigs develops in chapter iv, is created to interpret free reserves. Its sophisticated application to a mass of data underlies Meigs's major substantive finding: that free reserves would be an unreliable proximate objective for central-bank policy and are an unreliable indicator of either central-banking intentions or the probable future effects of central-banking actions. The reason free reserves are such an unreliable indicator is that what matters is not the actual level of free reserves but the difference between this level and the desired level. The two would be equivalent if desired free reserves were stable. In fact, however, they are not stable. Meigs isolates some of the variables affecting desired free reserves and estimates their quantitative effect: in particular, interest rates and seasonal influences. He demonstrates the existence of others—such as the effect of changes in Federal Reserve administration of discounting and tax effects in a number of years—without estimating in detail their quantitative effect.

Given the attention that has been lavished on free reserves by economists, bankers, and financial journalists, Meigs's substantive finding is of the greatest importance. It should and will have a significant impact on current thought and action. At the same time, it is a negative finding, a clearing of the underbrush. In consequence, I believe Meigs's longer run contribution will be very different.

If Meigs had started afresh to tackle the problem of the links between central-bank action and changes in the stock of money, I do not believe that he would have assigned free reserves the key role in his analysis. He was led to do so primarily by the emphasis that others have put on this magnitude. Now that he has demonstrated that this emphasis is misdirected, his organization of the problem and his techniques of analysis can be used to develop a more satisfactory understanding of the relation between Federal Reserve actions and the stock of money.

Meigs's analysis leads me to believe that such an analysis might well start from his finding that there is a close relation between changes in (1) unborrowed reserves corrected for altered reserve requirements and (2) member-bank deposits (see his Figure 3). The analysis might then work backward from the changes in (1) to their origins—in particular, to the factors altering required reserves and to the items other than open-market purchases and sales producing changes in unborrowed reserves. It might then work forward to explore the links between changes in (1) and (2), with special emphasis on a separate analysis of excess reserves and of borrowings. It might then proceed beyond member-bank deposits to the relation between such deposits, non-member bank deposits, and currency outside banks. I have already seen some work along these lines (in particular, a doctoral dissertation at the University of Minnesota by William Dewald, "Monetary Control and the Distribution of Money") and I predict that much more will follow.

Neither Meigs's analysis nor the more extensive analysis just sketched bears on what the ultimate objective of Federal Reserve policy should be: whether to produce a particular pattern of behavior of the stock of money or of interest rates or of prices or of employment or of still other magnitudes. Whatever this ultimate objective, Federal Reserve actions do affect the stock of money and it is clearly desirable that the Federal Reserve be able to predict what the effects will be, both to produce desired effects and, perhaps even more, to avoid undesired effects.

The Federal Reserve System has of course been well aware of the need for such understanding. It has done an enormous amount of research on these problems. It is the source to which all the rest of us must turn for the raw data with which to analyze the problems on our own and it has been unfailingly ready to produce such data and to make them available. This study, as Meigs explains in his acknowledgments, developed out of his own work at a Federal Reserve Bank and he drew heavily on the intellectual and statistical resources of the Bank.

For my own part, I am happy and proud to have had some part, if only as a matchmaker, in the fruitful multiple marriage which this monograph records between capital theory and banking analysis and between the practical concerns of the counting house and the academic concerns of the ivory tower. Long may such unions flourish.

MILTON FRIEDMAN

UNIVERSITY OF CHICAGO
May 7, 1962

Acknowledgments

THIS STUDY benefited very much from my association with the officers and other staff members of the Federal Reserve Bank of St. Louis. My colleagues of the Research Department who helped with their stock of Federal Reserve lore and their suggestions on the analytical problems involved were Homer Jones, William J. Abbott, Carl T. Arlt, Norman Bowsher, Leroy Grossman, Harry B. Kircher, David T. Lapkin, Clifton B. Luttrell, and Kornelis J. Walraven. I am deeply indebted to the late Guy Scott Freutel, gifted economist and friend, whose counsel and encouragement were of incalculable value.

During the 1958–59 academic year it was my great good fortune to be a member of the Workshop in Money and Banking at the University of Chicago. Milton Friedman supplied what turned out to be the key to the hypothesis of this study in a diagram jotted down in November, 1958. Others at the University who steered me away from pitfalls and made substantive contributions were Carl Christ, Reuben Kessel, David Meiselman, James Ford, Martin Bailey, Alvin L. Marty, John McCall, and George Morrison.

Allen G. Renz and William F. Burggrabe performed the computations with enthusiasm and resourcefulness. LaVerne Kunz marshaled the data, checked everything, and was otherwise indispensable. Pearl M. Lutteke made the charts. Constance Pfaff saw to it that all of the reference materials requested were on hand when needed. Marie Sullivan, Marie Fitzmaurice, and Anne O'Leary did the typing.

A special acknowledgment should go to my wife, Lester, and to Margaret, Susan, and Jimmy for being so patient with me during the writing of this "dissipation," as they aptly termed it.

It is needless to say that none of the people named above can be held responsible for any shortcomings or errors of the study. Furthermore, all statements or conclusions that might be considered to be comments on policies or methods of operation of the Federal Reserve System are my personal views and are not intended to represent views of anyone in the System.

Contents

I
Scope and Purposes of the Investigation

Introduction	1
Existing Theories of Money-Supply Determination	2
Purpose and Principal Hypothesis of This Study	3
Free Reserves as an Indicator of Monetary Policy	4
Plan of the Study	5

II
The Central Bank and the Deposit-Expansion Mechanism

Evolution of Reserve Position Doctrine	7
Lauchlin Currie's Extension of Reserve Position Theory	10
The Money-Supply Equation of Jan Tinbergen	11
Early Criticisms of Reserve Position Theory by C. O. Hardy and Seymour Harris	14
Keynes and Reserve Position Doctrine	18
Robert C. Turner's Study of Member-Bank Borrowing	19
The Interest-Reserves Relationship of Polak and White	21
Recent Free-Reserve Theory	23
Total Reserves and Deposit Expansion	24
The Excess Reserves of the 1930's	29
Some Conclusions from the Literature	30

III
The Accounting Framework and Some Preliminary Observations on Member-Bank Behavior

Derivation of Some Useful Accounting Identities	32
Some Preliminary Observations of Member-Bank Behavior	37

IV
Development of the Hypotheses

Introduction	42
Behavior of Individual Banks	42

Behavior of the System   44
The Treatment of Vault Cash   44
Determinants of the Free-Reserve Ratio   45
The Reserve-Adjustment Process   49
Influence of Changes in Unborrowed Reserves   53
Some Implications for Open-Market Operations   57
Control Characteristics of the Mechanism   58
Implications for Use of Free-Reserve Level as an Indicator of Mone-
    tary Policy   59
Determination of Market Interest Rates   60
Treatment of Excess Reserves and Borrowings Separately or as
    Combined in Free Reserves   62

V

Empirical Evidence

Introduction   64
Experiments in Predicting the Rate of Change of Deposits   66
Observations with Annual Data, 1929–59   66
Experiments with Monthly Data, 1947–58   69
Influence of the Excess Profits Tax in 1952 and 1953   72
Tests of the Period January, 1954, through December, 1959   73
Possible Explanations for a Shift in the Free Reserves-Interest Re-
    lationship   80
Some Implications of Time Lags for the Direction of Causation in
    the Free Reserves-Interest Relationship   82
Open-Market Operations and the Free-Reserve Ratio   83
Time Lags in the Influence of Open-Market Operations Upon Free
    Reserves   83

VI

Conclusions

Free Reserves as a Proximate Objective of Open-Market Operations   87
The Link between Open-Market Operations and Member-Bank Re-
    serve Positions   88
The Link between Reserve Positions and the Rate of Deposit Ex-
    pansion   90
Use of Total Reserves or Unborrowed Reserves as a Guide   92
Interpreting the Federal Reserve Statement   93

Appendixes

A. Regression Equations for Estimating Monthly Rates of Change
   of Deposits and Required Reserves   95
B. Regression Equation for Estimating Monthly Rates of Change
   of the Free-Reserve Ratio   98
C. Regression Equations for Estimating the Monthly Average
   Daily Free-Reserve Ratio   99
D. Data Employed in the Regression Equations   103

Bibliography

Bibliography   111

Index

Index   117

Illustrations

1. Rates of Change of Total Member-Bank Unborrowed Reserves and Total Member-Bank Deposits Subject to Reserve Requirements, February, 1947 through November, 1958   37
2. Member-Bank Reserve-Deposit Ratios, January, 1947 through December, 1958   38
3. Rates of Change of Total Member-Bank Deposits Subject to Reserve Requirements and of Total Unborrowed Reserves Adjusted for Changes in Average Reserve Requirement Ratio, January, 1947 through December, 1958   39
4. Rates of Change of Total Member-Bank Deposits Subject to Requirements and of Total Reserves Adjusted for Changes in the Average Reserve Requirement Ratio, January, 1947 through December, 1958   40
5. Long-Run Schedule of Desired Free-Reserve Ratios of All Member Banks as Market Interest Rates Vary   50
6. Schedules of Desired Rates of Change of the Free-Reserve Ratio for Given Actual Free-Reserve Ratios as Interest Rates Vary   53
7. Schedules of Rates of Change of Deposits and Unborrowed Reserves with Selected Free-Reserve Ratios as Market Interest Rates Vary   55
8. Observed and Predicted Monthly Rates of Change of Seasonally Adjusted Member-Bank Demand Deposits, 1947–1958   67
9. Observed and Predicted Monthly Rates of Change of Member-Bank Required Reserves, July, 1951–December, 1958   68
10. Annual Average Free-Reserve Ratios and Ratios of Bill Rates to New York Discount Rate, 1929–1959   69
11. Annual Average Free-Reserve Ratios and Ratios of Bill Rates to New York Discount Rate, 1929–1959, with Interest Ratios on Logarithmic Scale   70
12. Actual Free-Reserve Ratios and Ratios Predicted by Equation (T.14)   71
13. Actual Free-Reserve Ratios and Ratios Predicted by Equations (T.35) and (T.36)   75

14. Scatter Diagram of Bill Rates and Free-Reserve Ratios Adjusted to Rate of Change of Unborrowed Reserves, and First Approximation Curve Fitted to the Averages   76

15. Scatter Diagram of Rates of Change of Unborrowed Reserves and Free-Reserve Ratios Adjusted to the Bill Rate   78

16. Scatter Diagram of Bill Rates and Free-Reserve Ratios Adjusted to Rate of Change of Unborrowed Reserves and Seasonal Coefficients   79

I

Scope and Purposes of the Investigation

INTRODUCTION

AT VARIOUS TIMES it has been argued that the immediate goals of central-bank operations, in pursuing ultimate objectives of monetary policy, should be short-term interest rates, particular patterns of yields over a range of maturities, availability of credit, orderly conditions in the government securities markets, the rate of growth of the money supply, or some combination of these. From the constellation of suggested proximate goals, the money supply has been selected for attention here. Actually, the subject has been narrowed to the question: If Federal Reserve open-market operations are intended to produce a particular rate of growth or contraction of member-bank deposits, should the operations attempt to control the total reserves of the member banks or their free reserves?

When studies of money-supply determination are reviewed, two main theories emerge. One is that in general there is a stable relationship between the money supply and the reserve base, so that when the stock of reserves increases or decreases the money supply will change in a predictable way. According to this theory, therefore, a central bank can control the money supply by controlling total reserves of the banking and monetary system. The other main theory is that in the United States the volume of member-bank borrowing from the Federal Reserve System and the volume of excess reserves of the member banks (or the net of these two in "free" reserves) influence bank behavior in such a way that the rate of change of bank deposits and money supply can be predicted from these variables. An implication of the second main theory for the operation of a central bank is that attention should be focused on excess reserves and borrowings, or on free reserves, rather than on total reserves in attempting to control the money supply.

The principal conclusion of the study is that use of total member-bank reserves as a proximate goal for open-market operations would afford more precise control over the rate of bank-deposit expansion or contraction than would use of free reserves. Among the arguments, to be developed in more detail later on, are these: (1) The rate of change of deposits is closely related to the rate of change of total member-bank reserves but is not closely related to the level of free reserves; and (2)

1

the use of free-reserve targets may produce perverse results, such as contractions of bank credit and money supply in the early stages of recessions or unduly rapid expansions of deposits during recoveries.

EXISTING THEORIES OF MONEY-SUPPLY DETERMINATION

When the Federal Reserve System was established, it did not have a clear set of guides by which to control the money supply, nor were the existing theories of money-supply determination of much help in predicting the consequences of Federal Reserve action.[1] A number of able men within and outside the Federal Reserve System turned their attention to the problems of operating the new institution. Their efforts to distil comprehensible theories from a great mass of complex and often contradictory experience make fascinating reading. While some of what they said has proved in retrospect to be wrong, much that they observed is relevant today.

Early in its history the Federal Reserve experienced an apparent inability to control the total stock of member-bank reserves, or the volume of Federal Reserve credit outstanding, when it was discovered that the member banks tended to offset open-market operations with changes in the volume of their indebtedness to the Federal Reserve Banks. What will be called reserve position theory here was then developed as the rationale for attempting to control member-bank behavior through influencing the proportion of borrowed reserves in total reserves, since direct control of total reserves did not appear to be attainable. According to this theory, as member-bank indebtedness to the Federal Reserve increases, the banks are under increasing pressure to repay their borrowings and so become less willing to expand their earning assets and deposits. As they lose or gain reserves, as the result of System open-market operations or of changes in the market factors affecting reserves, they increase borrowings or repay in order to offset the losses or gains. Consequently, the theory implies, the Federal Reserve could control the rate of expansion or contraction of member-bank credit and deposits by conducting open-market operations so as to keep member-bank indebtedness or free reserves at some desired level.[2]

---

[1] For an excellent discussion of the Federal Reserve's search for guides, see Guy S. Freutel, "Income and Product Analysis for an Open Regional Economy: The Eighth Federal Reserve District" (Ph.D. diss., Department of Economics, Harvard University, 1956), pp. 1–106.

[2] Expressing the theory in terms of free reserves merely adds the influence of excess reserves to the earlier explanation in terms of borrowing. The term "free reserves" as used in this study means total member-bank excess reserves minus total member-bank borrowings from Federal Reserve Banks.

The two main theories are not so clearly alternative to one another as they might at first seem to be. Each contains useful insights regarding the behavior of the monetary system. If they are combined, each of them may contribute an essential element of a more satisfactory explanation of changes in money supply than can be obtained from either of them separately.

PURPOSE AND PRINCIPAL HYPOTHESIS OF THIS STUDY

One purpose of this study is to develop a way to incorporate variation in excess reserves and borrowings, or in the two as combined in free reserves, in a theory of money-supply determination. To simplify the problem, attention is focused upon the responses of the member banks of the Federal Reserve System to changes in the stock of unborrowed reserves—i.e., total reserves less borrowed reserves—in reserve requirements, in market interest rates, and in the discount rate. The responses to be explained by the theory are changes in excess reserves and borrowings (or free reserves) and the rate of change of total deposits. The analysis employed combines elements from the work of Riefler, Currie, Hardy, Turner, Tinbergen, Polak and White, Warburton, Friedman, and Meltzer, among others.[3]

The principal hypothesis of this study is that banks seek to maintain certain desired ratios of excess reserves and borrowings (or free reserves) to total deposits and that these desired ratios are functionally related to market interest rates and the discount rate. As interest rates and the supply of unborrowed reserves change, the actual ratios depart from the

[3] Winfield W. Riefler, *Money Rates and Money Markets in the United States* (New York: Harper & Bros., 1930); Lauchlin Currie, *The Supply and Control of Money in the United States* (Harvard Economic Studies, XLVII [2nd ed., rev.; Cambridge: Harvard University Press, 1935]); Charles O. Hardy, *Credit Policies of the Federal Reserve System* (Washington, D.C.: The Brookings Institution, 1932); Robert C. Turner, *Member-Bank Borrowing* (Columbus: Ohio State University, 1938); Jan Tinbergen, *Business Cycles in the United States of America 1919–1932* (Geneva: League of Nations, 1939), pp. 82–101; J. J. Polak and William H. White, "The Effect of Income Expansion on the Quantity of Money," *International Monetary Fund: Staff Papers*, IV, No. 3 (August, 1955), 398–433; Clark Warburton, "Bank Reserves and Business Fluctuations," *Journal of the American Statistical Association*, XLIII (December, 1948), 547–58, and "Monetary Velocity and Monetary Policy," *Review of Economics and Statistics*, XXX (November, 1948), 304–14; Milton Friedman, "Notes on Lectures in Price Theory" (mimeographed notes on lectures given January–June, 1951, in Economics 300*A* and 300*B*, at the University of Chicago), Part 2, pp. 112–114, and *A Program for Monetary Stability*, The Millar Lectures, Number Three, 1959 (New York: Fordham University Press, 1960); Allan H. Meltzer, "The Behavior of the French Money Supply: 1938–54," *Journal of Political Economy*, LXVII, No. 3 (June, 1959), 275–96.

desired ratios. In attempting to adjust the actual reserve ratios to the desired ratios, the banks increase or decrease their holdings of earning assets, thus causing deposits to change. The more the actual ratios diverge from the desired ratios the greater is the rate at which the banks attempt to adjust reserve positions and, hence, the greater is the rate of deposit change.

FREE RESERVES AS AN INDICATOR OF MONETARY POLICY

An additional objective of this study is to demonstrate the hazards of using the level of member-bank free reserves as an indicator of the "tightness" or "ease" of monetary policy. The theoretical apparatus and empirical evidence developed in this study provide strong support for recent criticisms of the free-reserve level as a monetary policy indicator or guide.[4] In particular, it will be demonstrated that a change in the absolute level of free reserves may be misleading as an indicator of the influence of Federal Reserve open-market operations on the rate of change of member-bank deposits. If an increase in the free-reserve level is to be interpreted as an easing in the restrictiveness of monetary policy, it ought to induce an increase in the rate of growth of member-bank deposits.[5] Actually, however, an increase in the free-reserve level may occur with a *reduction* in the rate of growth of deposits under certain conditions. For, according to the hypothesis of this study, it is not the absolute level of free reserves that is significant but the difference between actual free reserves and the volume of free reserves desired by banks. Efforts of banks to increase the free-reserve level may slow the rate of growth of deposits or bring about a contraction, as the banks sell assets in order to build up excess reserves and to pay off borrowings at the Federal Reserve.

[4] For an example of the use of free-reserve levels as an indicator of changes in monetary policy, see Hobart C. Carr, "Why and How to Read the Federal Reserve Statement," *Journal of Finance*, XIV, No. 4 (December, 1959), 504–19. For some recent discussions of the practice, see "The Significance and Limitations of Free Reserves," *Monthly Review*, Federal Reserve Bank of New York, November, 1958, pp. 162–67; Ralph A. Young, "Tools and Processes of Monetary Policy," *United States Monetary Policy* (New York: Columbia University, 1958), pp. 35–36; Milton Friedman, *A Program for Monetary Stability*, pp. 41–43.

[5] It is conceded that the rate of growth of the total money supply might conceivably increase when the rate of growth of member-bank deposits declines, so that the rate of growth of member-bank deposits is not by itself an adequate measure of the influence of Federal Reserve actions upon the money supply. However, the usual argument for using free reserves as an indicator is that the free-reserve level influences member-bank behavior. Therefore, an appropriate test based entirely on member-bank behavior should be possible.

PLAN OF THE STUDY

In chapter ii several studies of monetary system behavior will be reviewed to trace the origins of concepts employed in appraising them. In chapter iii some accounting identities will be derived as a framework for the later work, and preliminary observations of member-bank behavior in the postwar period will be made. In chapter iv the hypotheses of this study will be developed and some of their implications for the theory of money-supply determination will be discussed. Chapter v will report on empirical work done in testing the hypotheses, and the conclusions will be stated in chapter vi.

II

The Central Bank and the Deposit-Expansion Mechanism

IN THE 1920's and early 1930's, before monetary theory was eclipsed by the income-expenditure theories of Keynes, there was much interest in how the deposit-expansion process worked and in how central banks wielded their influence. The classic treatment of the multiple expansion principle by C. A. Phillips appeared in 1920.[1] John Maynard Keynes published *A Tract on Monetary Reform* in 1923 and followed it with *A Treatise on Money* in 1930.[2] Also in 1930, Winfield Riefler crystallized doctrines of the Federal Reserve System in his *Money Rates and Money Markets in the United States*.[3] *The Supply and Control of Money in the United States*, by Lauchlin Currie, was published in 1934.[4] These works and many others of the period are rich sources of information and interpretation regarding central bank experience. In the 1950's, a resurgence of interest in monetary theory and policy brought a new wave of studies of how central banks influence bank behavior and the money supply.[5] Without attempting to make a comprehensive review of Federal Reserve history or the evolution of central-bank doctrine, this part of the paper

[1] C. A. Phillips, *Bank Credit* (New York: Macmillan Co., 1921).

[2] John Maynard Keynes, *A Tract on Monetary Reform* (London: Macmillan Co., 1923) and *A Treatise on Money* (2 vols.; New York: Harcourt, Brace & Co., 1930).

[3] Winfield W. Riefler, *Money Rates and Money Markets in the United States* (New York: Harper & Bros., 1930).

[4] Lauchlin Currie, *The Supply and Control of Money in the United States* (2d ed., rev.; Cambridge: Harvard University Press, 1935).

[5] Major studies underway in 1961 include: Milton Friedman and Anna J. Schwartz, *The Money Stock of the United States, 1867–1960* (to be published in 1962 by the National Bureau of Economic Research, Inc.); a monograph on determinants of the United States money supply, 1875–1955, by Phillip Cagan, also at the National Bureau of Economic Research; a book by James Tobin, of the Cowles Commission and the President's Council of Economic Advisers; and a study by Karl Brunner at U.C.L.A. (For a preliminary report see his "Some Major Problems in Monetary Theory" *American Economic Review*, LI, No. 2 [May, 1961], 47–56). The work of Clark Warburton bridges the gap between the literature of the 1930's and the new outpouring. In his studies of the influence of money-supply changes on economic activity, he has also dealt with how the money supply is determined. See in particular his "Monetary Control under the Federal Reserve Act," *Political Science Quarterly*, LXI (December, 1946), 505–34.

mines the literature new and old for theories and evidence bearing on the question whether Federal Reserve open-market operations could most effectively control the money supply through influencing total reserves of the member banks or through influencing excess reserves and borrowings.

EVOLUTION OF RESERVE POSITION DOCTRINE

Although experience of the Bank of England and other central banks could be looked to for precedents and doctrines when the Federal Reserve Banks opened for business, the American system with its thousands of individual member banks was believed to be unique in many ways. Appearing to confirm the uniqueness of the American system, a perplexing problem arose in 1922 when the Federal Reserve Banks attempted to build up their earning assets by purchasing securities in the open market. As the open-market purchases were made, the member banks reduced their borrowings from the Reserve Banks by about the amount of the System purchases, leaving total Reserve Bank credit virtually unchanged. When securities were sold in 1923 member-bank borrowing increased, again leaving total Reserve Bank credit about the same. The unexpected reactions of the banks to System open-market operations did more than present a problem in financing the operations of the new institutions; they cast doubt upon the effectiveness of the discount rate as a central-bank instrument. If the volume of discounting was independent of the discount rate, how could the central bank be effective? The response of the Federal Reserve System to this challenge was a new doctrine, called reserve position doctrine here, that elevated open-market operations to the commanding position held by bank rate in other countries.[6]

The 1923 Annual Report of the Federal Reserve Board discussed open-market operations and discounting at some length, stating that there was a causal link between them:

The part that open-market operations may play in general credit policy is influenced by the fact that changes in the volume of securities held by the reserve banks have an effect on the volume of their discounts for member banks.

---

[6] Lester Chandler has a good account of the early days of reserve position doctrine in his *Benjamin Strong, Central Banker* (Washington, D.C.: The Brookings Institution, 1958), pp. 237–40. Perhaps the earliest discussion in a Federal Reserve publication appeared in the *Tenth Annual Report of the Federal Reserve Board Covering Operations for the Year 1923*, pp. 3–16. Winfield W. Riefler made the most complete early statement of the doctrine and subjected its hypotheses to careful testing in his *Money Rates and Money Markets*. Other early writers on the doctrine were W. Randolph Burgess, *The Reserve Banks and the Money Market* (Rev. ed.; New York: Harper & Bros., 1936); and Irving Fisher, *The Theory of Interest* (New York: Kelley & Millman, Inc., 1954), pp. 444–51.

The purchase of securities in the open market by a Federal reserve bank places funds in the hands of member banks which these banks may use in the repayment of borrowings from the reserve banks; the sale of securities, on the other hand, by withdrawing funds from the market may lead to additional borrowing from the reserve banks.[7]

It was further observed that the relationship was based upon experience of the System as a whole and was not evident to the same extent in the operations of the individual banks. Therefore it was necessary that open-market operations be made a matter of System policy.[8]

The observed facts of the early 1920's that the new theory sought to explain were these: (1) When banks lost reserves because of gold flows, currency drains, or Federal Reserve open-market operations, they increased their borrowing from the Reserve Banks; (2) when they gained reserves, they reduced their borrowing; and (3) high levels of borrowing were associated with high short-term interest rates and vice versa. Two hypotheses were drawn by the originators of reserve position doctrine to explain the facts. The first was that reserve losses cause banks to increase their borrowing and reserve gains cause them to reduce borrowing. The second was that high levels of member-bank borrowing cause short-term market interest rates to be high, and low levels of borrowing cause market rates to be low. Underlying both hypotheses was an assumption that banks are reluctant to be in debt. Consequently, according to the doctrine, banks borrow only when they must and the volume of their borrowing is affected very little, if at all, by changes in profitability or cost. As Dr. Riefler said:

> In other words, to the extent that member banks have hesitated to borrow from the reserve banks during this period and have repaid their indebtedness as soon as possible, one would expect to find—as one does in fact find—that loans were most costly in the money markets when borrowing at the reserve banks was large, and that funds have been offered most freely when indebtedness at the reserve banks was low.[9]

Implications for the conduct of open-market operations were stated by W. Randolph Burgess as follows:

> The principle of open-market operations may be summarized by saying that purchases of securities by Reserve Banks tend to relieve member banks from debt to the Reserve Banks, and lead them to adopt a more liberal lending and investing policy. Money rates become easier; bank deposits increase. . . . Con-

[7] *Tenth Annual Report of the Federal Reserve Board Covering Operations for the Year 1923*, pp. 13, 3–16.

[8] *Ibid.*, p. 15.

[9] Riefler, *Money Rates and Money Markets*, p. 26.

versely, sales of securities by the Reserve Banks increase member bank borrowing and lead the banks to adopt a somewhat less liberal policy. Money rates grow firmer; bank deposits tend to decline.[10]

The first hypothesis is especially interesting because it suggests that direct control of deposit expansion through control of the total volume of bank reserves might be unattainable, for changes in member-bank borrowing would automatically offset open-market operations intended to change total reserves.

The theory that money market rates are determined by the level of borrowings appears to have grown out of an earlier one that related rates to the volume of excess reserves of the New York banks. When excess reserves were large, the banks were said to lend freely and interest rates were low; when excess reserves were low, rates were said to be high. According to Burgess, the figure for excess reserves of the New York banks lost much of its significance when the Federal Reserve System was established because the banks no longer carried excess reserves, relying on the Reserve Banks in emergencies. "The fluctuating element became the total amount of credit advanced by the Reserve Banks. When the demand for funds was large the banks borrowed more from the Reserve Banks or sold them acceptances, and when the demand decreased, this borrowing was reduced or the acceptances ran off."[11]

To support the assertion that member-bank borrowing was not governed primarily by opportunities for profit, Dr. Riefler demonstrated that differences between market rates and the discount rate persisted. Whenever market rates rose above the discount rate, he argued, the banks would have borrowed enough funds for relending to bring market rates back down to the discount rate, if they had not been reluctant to borrow. This is essentially what they did do in the case of acceptances, the rates for which seldom moved appreciably away from the New York Reserve Bank buying rate, he said.[12]

As evidence of the influence of borrowing on interest rates, Dr. Riefler showed that month-to-month changes in a weighted average of short-term money rates corresponded closely with changes in the average volume of member-bank indebtedness when the two were plotted together

[10] Burgess, *The Reserve Banks and the Money Market*, p. 239.

[11] Burgess, *The Reserve Banks and the Money Market*, p. 317. See also Burgess, "Factors Affecting Changes in Short Term Interest Rates," *Journal of the American Statistical Association*, XXII (June, 1927), 195–201; and Irving Fisher, *The Theory of Interest*, pp. 444–51.

[12] Riefler, *Money Rates and Money Markets*, pp. 20–28.

and that the correspondence was free of any lag.[13] He concluded that the net effect of various monetary factors, including gold movements, changes in currency demand, and Federal Reserve open-market operations, was registered in the current indebtedness of the member banks and that changes in this indebtedness appeared to be the initiating force in changes of money rates.[14]

LAUCHLIN CURRIE'S EXTENSION OF RESERVE POSITION THEORY

Lauchlin Currie attempted to extend reserve position theory to prediction of changes in net demand deposits. The earlier discussion, by Riefler, Burgess, Seymour Harris, and others, had been largely concerned with the influence of bank indebtedness upon market interest rates, touching only incidentally upon changes in deposits.

Currie agreed with Dr. Riefler that profitability was apparently not of much influence upon the volume of borrowing, for the bulk of loans and investments had usually yielded more than the cost of borrowing. If profitability had been the main consideration, he said, borrowing would have expanded continuously.[15] For the period 1922 through 1931 he also found that the movement of net demand deposits for all member banks was generally in inverse relation to the movement in member-bank borrowing.[16] The relationship, however, was neither invariable nor uniform.

The lack of uniformity in the borrowings-deposits relationship Currie explained in part by a hypothesis that banks are not uniformly sensitive to indebtedness, arguing that, "if, at any time, the bulk of the borrowing has been contracted by banks that are not sensitive, less contraction of demand deposits is to be expected than would have taken place if the borrowing had been done by a class of banks highly sensitive."[17] He tested the hypothesis by studying movements of deposits and borrowings for three classes of banks: New York banks, other large banks throughout the country, and country banks. Of the three classes, he concluded, the New York banks were the most sensitive, for an increase in their borrowing was invariably followed by a decrease in deposits. The country banks were least sensitive, never really getting out of debt as a class.[18]

An additional explanation for the lack of uniformity in the borrowings-deposits relationship, according to Currie, was that the banks might not

---

[13] *Ibid.*, Chart VI, p. 26. Deviations from the averages, expressed in multiples of standard deviations, were plotted for the period from August, 1917 to August, 1928.

[14] *Ibid.*, pp. 26–27.

[15] Currie, *The Supply and Control of Money*, pp. 84–89.

[16] *Ibid.*, Chart II, pp. 90–91.

[17] *Ibid.*, p. 91.

[18] *Ibid.*, Charts II, VII, pp. 92–96.

be equally sensitive to indebtedness at all times. He had noticed, in particular, the following discrepancies:

An increase of over $400 million in rediscounts in 1923 corresponded with a slight decrease in deposits; an equal increase in 1925 was followed by an increase in deposits. A level of around $600 million in rediscounts corresponded with a cessation in the growth of deposits in 1926; in 1928–29, however, a level of around $1 billion was accompanied by only a slight contraction of deposits. Banks expanded their deposits while still over $400 million in debt, in 1927; they contracted deposits from the middle of 1930 to the middle of 1931 when indebtedness was only around $200 million.[19]

As might be expected, he said, the desire to be out of debt probably varies with the business cycle.

In the upswing, bank assets are in good shape, the need for liquidity does not seem so pressing, and the profitableness of borrowing is large. In the downswing, on the other hand, the quality of bank assets tends to deteriorate, borrowing becomes less profitable, confidence diminishes, bank runs increase, and there is naturally, a desire for greater liquidity.[20]

In sum, Currie may be said to have concluded that the banks' desire to reduce indebtedness was what made open-market operations effective in controlling deposits. He charged the Federal Reserve authorities with not gauging well enough the influence of member-bank indebtedness upon deposits, however, saying that in 1928 and in 1931–32 policies resulting in high levels of borrowing produced undesired contractions in deposits.[21]

THE MONEY-SUPPLY EQUATION OF JAN TINBERGEN

In his study of the business cycle in the United States for the period 1919–32 Tinbergen derived a money-supply equation involving short-term interest rates and the net indebtedness of the member banks, which was based on the Riefler-Burgess version of reserve position theory.[22] Denoting total money supply by M, currency outside banks by C_O, and total bank deposits (member and nonmember) by D, he had:[23]

$$M = C_O + D. \qquad (2.1)$$

---

[19] *Ibid.*, p. 96.   [20] *Ibid.*, p. 97.   [21] *Ibid.*, p. 101.

[22] A brief discussion can be found in Jan Tinbergen, *Econometrics* (New York: Blakiston Co., 1951), pp. 138–41. The complete version appears in Tinbergen, *Business Cycles in the United States of America, 1919–1932*, pp. 82–88. The latter source is the one cited here. Incidentally, the earliest use of a net borrowed reserve concept (or net free) that I was able to find in the literature was in Tinbergen's work.

[23] The symbols used in this study have been substituted for those used by Professor Tinbergen in all of the equations of this section. In the Tinbergen equations the variables are expressed in terms of deviations from their respective means rather than in their absolute values.

He combined bank vault cash, C_V, with currency outside banks, C_O, in accordance with the Federal Reserve definition of "currency in circulation," and assumed that, for both currency outside banks and vault cash, supply follows demand automatically so that only demand need be considered.[24]

The key assumption appears in the following passage:

In principle, the supply of deposits may be said to be regulated by acts of price fixation—i.e., fixation of the short-term interest rate [r_s]—by the commercial banks, on the basis of their debt position with the Federal Reserve Banks. The fact that debts (in the form of rediscounts) are permitted to be incurred only for a short period creates a tendency for the banks to fix their interest rates in such a way as to avoid such debts. This means that the higher the net debt position, indicated by bills rediscounted [R_B] minus excess reserves [R_E], the higher the rate fixed.[25]

In a footnote he cited Riefler's *Money Rates and Money Markets* in regard to the assumed relationship of interest rates and indebtedness. The relationship was expressed as

$$r_s = f(R_B - R_E) . \qquad (2.2)$$

One reference to the discount rate appeared in a footnote to the passage quoted above: "One might, moreover, have expected to find an influence exercised by the gold stock—viz., a raising of discount rates when the gold cover of the liabilities of the Federal Reserve Banks becomes low. However, no evidence of such an influence is found."[26]

When short-term interest rates and the net indebtedness of the banks were plotted in a scatter diagram, he found that in the years in which borrowings exceeded excess reserves the rate of interest rose steeply as indebtedness increased. Nearly all of the points for the period covered by the study were in the net borrowed portion of the diagram. A straight line fitted to the scatter for the years 1919–32 was then used to approximate the function of (2.2):

$$r_s = 4(R_B - R_E) . \qquad (2.3)$$

The factor 4 indicated that the banks raised their interest rate by 1 per cent when their indebtedness to the Federal Reserve increased by $250 million.[27]

[24] Tinbergen, *Business Cycles*, p. 83.

[25] *Ibid.* The symbols in brackets were substituted for symbols which appeared in parentheses in the original.

[26] *Ibid.*, fn. 3.

[27] *Ibid.*, p. 84.

From a simplified balance sheet of the Federal Reserve System the determinants of the net indebtedness were derived:

$$R_B - R_E = R_R + C_O + C_V - (G + P) . \qquad (2.4)$$

Federal Reserve holdings of securities, P, and the gold stock, G, were considered to be autonomous variables in the determination of the supply of deposits. Currency in circulation, $C_O + C_V$, was considered to be determined by demand and also to be beyond the control of the banking authorities.

Required reserves were technically related to total deposits through the prescribed reserve requirements, and these were assumed to be equivalent to a linear relation:[28]

$$R_R = \mu D . \qquad (2.5)$$

The price fixation equation for r_s was then written as

$$r_s = 4[\mu D + C_O + C_V - (G + P)] , \qquad (2.6)$$

or, according to (2.1)

$$r_s = 4[\mu M + (1 - \mu)C_O + C_V - (G + P)] . \qquad (2.7)$$

When (2.7) was solved with respect to M, the supply equation for money became

$$M = \frac{r_s}{4\mu} - \frac{1}{\mu}[(1 - \mu)C_O + C_V - (G + P)] . \qquad (2.8)$$

Since μ had been estimated to be 0.038, the supply equation for M was

$$M = 6.6\,r_s - 25\,C_O - 26\,C_V + 26(G + P) . \qquad (2.9)$$

Some interesting implications of the Tinbergen theory of money-supply determination appear when equations (2.7) and (2.9) are examined term by term, remembering that all of the variables are expressed as deviations from their respective means. Equation (2.7) says, in effect, that a given change in money supply, with autonomously determined changes in currency in circulation, gold stock, and Federal Reserve securities holdings, would require a particular increase or decrease in member-bank indebtedness. The change in net indebtedness is merely the residual required to complete an accounting identity. Since an increase of $250 million of indebtedness had been found by correlation to be associated with a 1 per

[28] Because of the problems of deposit shifts among banks subject to different reserve requirements, μ was estimated by correlation of R_R with D and a trend. By this method it was found to be 0.038 (*ibid.*, p. 87).

cent increase in the short-term interest rate, the interest rate, r_s, was thus determined.

Equation (2.7) might be used to state the Riefler-Burgess hypothesis that System open-market operations and changes in the market factors affecting reserves determine the level of member-bank borrowing and the short-term interest rate. It implies that there is a certain quantity of bank credit demanded and that this quantity, measured here by deposits, will be supplied by the banking system. Given the reserve balances provided by currency flows, gold flows, and open-market operations of the Federal Reserve System, the banks will borrow whatever additional reserves are required in order to supply the quantity of credit demanded. Open-market operations of the Federal Reserve then influence market interest rates by determining the size of the residual "need" for reserves that the banks must meet by discounting. Because the banks are reluctant to borrow, they raise the interest rates they charge as their indebtedness increases. This in turn influences the quantity of credit demanded by changing its cost. This particular version of reserve position theory thus is not so much a theory of money-supply determination as it is a theory to explain central-bank control over interest rates. This is of course implied by what Dr. Riefler said in his preface:

Whether central banks confine themselves to protecting the exchanges and forestalling panics, or under a broader conception of these functions undertake to stabilize business and control price levels, their chief instrument of action is the price charged for credit, and they must endeavor to accomplish these objectives mainly by bringing their influence to bear on money rates.[29]

Equation (2.9), however, could be interpreted in a quite different way, to say that money supply is determined by the amounts of reserves provided by system open-market purchases, gold flows, currency flows, and borrowing. The amount of borrowing is determined by the short-term interest rate. Therefore, open-market operations intended to produce particular desired changes in the money supply would have to allow for the amounts of reserves the banks would be expected to borrow, or to repay, as interest rates vary.

EARLY CRITICISMS OF RESERVE POSITION THEORY
BY C. O. HARDY AND SEYMOUR HARRIS

As experience with the Federal Reserve System accumulated, facts were observed which did not appear to fit the reserve position theory, especially from 1927 on. Dr. Riefler pointed out exceptions to one of the basic assumptions, saying,

[29] Riefler, *Money Rates and Money Markets*, pp. xi–xii.

It is, moreover, quite inconceivable that, in a system as widespread as the Federal reserve system with its thousands of member banks, there should be no borrowing whatever governed predominantly by motives of profit. Indeed, it seems highly probable that member banks when they borrow and when they adjust their operations to repay their borrowing are affected to a certain extent by its cost in relation to money rates in the market.[30]

He also described the way a member bank's choice between borrowing or calling loans to meet a temporary reserve deficiency was influenced by whether the call rate was above or below the discount rate.[31] C. O. Hardy and Seymour Harris, in their reviews of Federal Reserve operations through the early 1930's, discussed numerous episodes that were not easily explained by the reserve position theory in its early form, and Robert C. Turner challenged directly the assumption that borrowing is not influenced by interest rates.

Charles O. Hardy was concerned with the effectiveness of Federal Reserve control over member-bank reserve balances rather than with control over member-bank borrowing. He believed that the tradition against borrowing had made changes of discount rate ineffective as a means for controlling member-bank balances through influencing the volume of borrowing and so open-market operations had become the most important tool of the Federal Reserve.[32] He observed, as had Riefler, Burgess, and Currie, that when the banks gain reserves from open-market operations they tend to apply new reserves first to paying off their borrowings, and that when they lose reserves they borrow, at least temporarily, to replenish their reserves.[33] He differed from Riefler and Burgess, however, by regarding such induced changes in borrowing as impediments to the effectiveness of open-market operations.[34] They, on the other hand, had considered changes in member-bank borrowing to be proximate objectives of open-market operations.

When Hardy examined four instances in which he said the Federal Reserve had tried to increase the volume of credit outstanding by buying securities and two instances in which attempts had been made to contract credit by selling, he found a high degree of correspondence between open-market operations and the direction of change of member-bank reserves. Repayment of indebtedness, and sometimes gold movements, tended to work against the changes in Federal Reserve holdings of securities, he

---

[30] Riefler, *Money Rates and Money Markets*, p. 34.

[31] *Ibid.*, pp. 34–35.

[32] Hardy, *Credit Policies of the Federal Reserve System*, pp. 228–32.

[33] *Ibid.*, pp. 231–32.

[34] *Ibid.*, pp. 233–34.

said, but these offsets were not great enough to cancel the effect of open-market operations. He also concluded that bank investments showed a pronounced change in the same direction as Federal Reserve holdings of securities in every case, but that bank loans showed no responsiveness.[35]

Characteristics of the deposit-expansion mechanism were summed up by Hardy as follows:

1. The chain of causal relationships which it is desired to set up would run from open market policy to the reserves of member banks; thence to loans and investments on the one hand and deposits on the other; and finally to the buying policy of the public and the price level.

2. The first effect of reversal of open market policy is to stimulate a partial offsetting change in rediscounts (which is apparently not influenced significantly by rediscount rates).

3. A second probable effect (less certain to occur) is to divert the demand for funds for reserve purposes from the Reserve Banks to the foreign market, or vice versa, causing gold to flow in or out.

4. These offsets are not complete, however. Reserves of member banks do show some response to changes in open market policy.

5. Member banks' investment policy responds readily to an open market policy which is designed to further either expansion or contraction.

6. Loans at member banks do not show a tendency to expand and contract as Federal Reserve policy grows more and less liberal.[36]

It is evident that Hardy expressed a reserve position theory, with changes in member-bank reserve balances as the instrument through which the Federal Reserve could control the quantity of credit. Like Currie, he rejected the assumption of a constant desired reserve position, saying,

The state of business sentiment affects the problem of credit control by de-termining the volume of currency which will be readily kept in circulation, the proportion of cash to bank deposits held by the public, *and the relative extent to which funds put into the banks by Reserve system operations will be used to support increased deposit liabilities or sent back to the Reserve Banks in repayment of borrowings.*[37] [Italics mine.]

Seymour Harris drew attention to periods in which the inverse rela-tionship between changes in Federal Reserve holdings of securities and in member-bank indebtedness, which was a principal element of the early reserve position theory, did not appear to be very close.[38] Even in the

[35] *Ibid.*, pp. 233–36.

[36] *Ibid.*, p. 236.

[37] *Ibid.*, pp. 238–39.

[38] Harris, *Twenty Years of Federal Reserve Policy*, pp. 175–85, 256–65, 440–41, 493–98, 509–51, 615–31.

relatively stable years 1922–25, in which the theory had been developed, the relationship was not close, he said.[39] There also were considerable discrepancies in 1927–29, in part because of gold flows and currency drains that offset Federal Reserve open-market operations, according to Harris.[40] In 1930–32 reduction of member-bank indebtedness did not halt the decline in bank deposits.[41]

From his review of Federal Reserve operations Harris drew several main conclusions about reserve position theory, especially regarding the implications for the effectiveness of open-market operations. One obstacle to the effectiveness of reductions of indebtedness as a way to increase the supply of credit which he described is that indebtedness may decline rapidly in the financial centers while declining more slowly elsewhere. Surplus funds accumulate in the financial centers before the country banks are out of debt so that the reserves provided by open-market operations do not necessarily go either to banks heavily in debt or to communities especially in need of a stimulus.[42]

Banks also prefer to remain in debt when it is profitable to do so, according to Harris.[43]

In fact, they do borrow to relend at a profit although it is not always easy to discover such violations of the code. Open market rates . . . , almost throughout the history of the Federal Reserve System, have been above Bank rates, and customers' rates have been far above those of the open market. It is, therefore, misleading to argue that member banks do not borrow to lend at a profit. In fact, they are using reserve funds to extend their business, and even banks in debt but a few days at intervals are using reserve resources for this purpose. When the subject of reserve requirements was under discussion, it was not appreciated that member banks would economize on reserves under the new system in that they would dispense with surplus reserves and depend on reserve banks to meet their temporary deficits. Member banks have obtained concessions not anticipated by Congress in that that they have kept less till money than was predicted and have retained virtually no surplus cash. Several billions

[39] *Ibid.*, pp. 179–80.

[40] *Ibid.*, pp. 181–85. It should be recognized, however, that the theory, as expounded in Dr. Riefler's book, did not overlook the influence of gold flows, Treasury operations, and currency flows. It was the net change in the market factors *plus* Federal Reserve open-market operations that was deemed to influence the level of borrowing, rather than changes in Federal Reserve securities holdings alone. Development of reserve factor analysis within the Federal Reserve System in the 1920's is evidence of the attention given to other factors. See Riefler, *Money Rates and Money Markets*, Appendix II, pp. 237–59.

[41] Harris, *Twenty Years of Federal Reserve Policy*, pp. 618–25.

[42] *Ibid.*, pp. 619–20.   [43] *Ibid.*, pp. 256–61, 513.

of investments of member banks are made on the basis of temporary (and to some extent permanent) loans by the reserve banks; for the system as a whole, these temporary loans constitute a permanent advance of appreciable proportions.[44]

The theory of the influence of member-bank borrowing upon market interest rates, Harris said, might better be expressed as follows:

In the prewar days, fluctuations in the surplus reserves of clearing banks were observed with interest by all those who were interested in the state of the money market, for the approach of an exhaustion of the surplus was an announcement of impending restriction. In a similar manner, it might be stated that a large volume of indebtedness is reflected in higher money rates, because member banks cannot continue to borrow from reserve banks indefinitely. Restrictive measures follow large increases in indebtedness, not so much because member banks refuse to stay in debt, but because a large volume of indebtedness is an announcement that large additional resources will not be available.[45]

The principal suggestion by Harris for increasing the effectiveness of open-market operations was that more attention might be paid to controlling the reserve balances of the member banks and less to their indebtedness. He argued that if this had been done in 1922–25, the period in which the borrowings doctrine had been developed, it would have been discovered that monetary conditions are influenced by the cash assets of the banks as well as by the extent of the banks' indebtedness.[46]

KEYNES AND RESERVE POSITION DOCTRINE

Observing the American experiment from abroad, Keynes dissented from several of the interpretations drawn by Federal Reserve authorities.[47] Especially did he question the existence of a strong tradition against borrowing on the part of American banks. To the contrary, he argued that one of the most important differences between the American and British systems was that borrowing from the central bank was far greater in volume and more frequent in America than in Britain, at least in the early days of the Federal Reserve. "There is all the difference in the world between a system in which, to adopt London parlance, the market is habitually 'in' the Bank to a certain extent as in America, and one in which it is only 'in' the Bank temporarily or as a last resort when it has been taken by surprise, as in London," he said.[48] The Federal Re-

---

[44] *Ibid.*, p. 261.
[45] *Ibid.*, p. 264. See also discussion of Burgess, pp. 8–9, above.
[46] *Ibid.*, p. 189.
[47] Keynes, *A Treatise on Money*, II, 234–61.
[48] *Ibid.*, p. 235.

serve practices of permitting discount rates to be lower than short-term market rates much of the time and of buying acceptances at rates below the discount rate seriously weakened the power of the new central bank to control total member-bank reserves, in his opinion. Accordingly,

The history of the Federal Reserve System since the war has been, first of all, a great abuse of the latitude thus accorded to the Member Banks to increase the "advances" of the Reserve Banks, and subsequently a series of efforts by the Reserve authorities to invent gadgets and conventions which shall give them a power, more nearly similar to that which the Bank of England has, without any overt alteration of the law.[49]

Keynes also gave short shrift to the argument, central to reserve position doctrine, that changes in member-bank borrowing automatically offset System open-market operations. Data provided by Randolph Burgess on this point, he argued, showed merely that when open-market operations were large they were apt to be partially offset by changes in borrowing.[50] Thus he was substantially in agreement with the views of C. O. Hardy discussed earlier.

Robert C. Turner's Study of Member-Bank Borrowing

Riefler, Burgess, Currie, and Hardy, as we have seen, were willing virtually to write off the discount rate as a means for controlling the volume of member-bank reserves. Robert C. Turner was not; in his study of member-bank borrowing, he attempted to determine whether banks were in fact so insensitive to the cost of borrowing that use of bank rate would be ineffective. In place of the "need" theory of borrowing, which had been used to justify dethroning the discount rate, he expressed a "profit" theory:

When faced with a deficit (or excess) in reserves, banks will adjust their reserve position either through increasing (or decreasing) borrowings, or decreasing (or increasing) open-market loans, and the decision will rest upon the relative costliness of the two alternatives, to the effect that the volume of borrowing will be a function of the profitability of open-market loans relative to the discount rate. [Italics in the original.][51]

He did not, however, believe that banks felt free to borrow without limit whenever possibilities of profit occurred. Instead, he believed there was a limit to the debt a bank was willing to incur, a limit that probably was a function of such variables as the size and location of the bank, phase of the business cycle, and other factors in addition to profitability. Thus, if

[49] *Ibid.*, p. 239.
[50] *Ibid.*, pp. 257–58.
[51] Turner, *Member-Bank Borrowing*, p. 96.
(1938)

market interest rates were to go considerably above the discount rate, banks could borrow for profit without necessarily bringing market rates back into line with the discount rate, and if market rates were to fall below the discount rate, banks might stop borrowing altogether without bringing market rates back up to the discount rate.[52]

To test the profit theory of borrowing, Turner correlated the volume of borrowing with the spread between the discount rate and various market rates of interest by months for the period 1922 through 1936, for the system as a whole and for the individual Federal Reserve Districts.[53] He concluded that the profit theory appeared to provide a partial explanation of changes in the volume of borrowing. Although borrowings tended to increase as the profit spread increased, there seemed to be a limit beyond which borrowings did not readily go, despite further increases in profitability. This he interpreted to mean that the tradition against borrowing comes gradually into play as borrowing increases. In every district, and for every time interval tested, movements in the profit spread tended either to coincide with or to precede changes in borrowings. In the New York, Chicago, and Boston districts no time lag between changes in profit spread and changes in discounts could be detected in the monthly data he used. In other districts, however, Turner found a tendency for discounts to lag behind changes in profit spread by one or two months.[54]

Turner then outlined a general theory of borrowing, using the following accounting identities to relate total reserves (R), borrowed reserves (R_B), unborrowed reserves (R_U), required reserves (R_R), and excess reserves (R_E):[55]

$$R_U = R - R_B , \qquad (2.10)$$

and

$$R_U = R_R + R_E - R_B . \qquad (2.11)$$

Just as in this study, R_U is the sum of the sources and uses of reserves which are not within the control of the banks, including the gold stock, currency in circulation, Treasury balances, and Federal Reserve holdings of securities. On the right-hand side of equation (2.11) are the factors that are amenable to member-bank control, required reserves, excess reserves, and borrowings.

An adequate theory of borrowing according to Turner, would include

[52] *Ibid.*, pp. 89–90.

[53] *Ibid.*, pp. 97–144.

[54] *Ibid.*, p. 154.

[55] *Ibid.*, pp. 145–60. For convenience in exposition here the symbols used in this study have been substituted for those used by Turner.

the net effect of changes in the factors summarized in R_U above, as well as profitability of borrowing, the tradition against borrowing, custom, habit, knowledge of opportunities, personal attitudes, and the need for borrowing, which was defined as "a need growing out of the demands of customers for working-capital loans or for the maintenance of bank secondary reserves."[56]

If the factors most stressed by Turner are singled out, his theory of borrowing might be stated as follows:

$$\Delta R_B = f(\Delta R_U, R_B, r_m - r_d) . \qquad (2.12)$$

A change in R_U forces the banks to adjust. The amount of the resulting change in borrowing then depends upon the current level of borrowing (R_B) and the spread between the discount rate (r_d) and the market rate on paper used by banks as an alternative to borrowing (r_m). The influence of the current level of borrowing incorporates the influence of the tradition against borrowing for, according to Turner, as borrowing increases the tradition becomes more and more operative, tending to restrain further increases. He pointed out in support of this assumption that in 1929, when the profit spread on open-market loans increased to great heights, borrowing remained high but did not increase in proportion to the increase in profit spread.[57]

THE INTEREST-RESERVES RELATIONSHIP OF POLAK AND WHITE

As part of their study, "The Effect of Income Expansion on the Quantity of Money," J. J. Polak and William H. White derived a relationship between short-term interest rates and desired free reserves of the member banks.[58] They assumed that the banks "want to balance the convenience of a high reserve ratio against a low rate of interest, the inconvenience and risk of a lower ratio against a higher rate of interest."[59] Because some of the excess reserves of the banks have been obtained by borrowing from the Federal Reserve and because indebtedness is considered undesirable, net excess reserves, defined as excess reserves minus borrowings, were the ones they used for comparison with interest rates.

---

[56] *Ibid.*, p. 156.

[57] *Ibid.*, p. 155. See also Polakoff, *Journal of Finance*, XV (March, 1960), 1–18, for a study of member-bank borrowing in the period 1953–58; and Warren L. Smith, "The Discount Rate as a Credit-Control Weapon," *Journal of Political Economy*, XLVI (April, 1958), 171–77.

[58] Polak and White, *International Monetary Fund Staff Papers*, IV (August, 1955), 398–433.

[59] *Ibid.*, p. 422.

Polak and White expressed net excess reserves as a ratio to total deposits, arguing that the need for net excess reserves could be taken as proportional to the volume of deposit liabilities. Reserves are desired as a cushion between variations in actual reserves and required reserves, they said, and these variations are proportional to the volume of deposit liabilities, since larger deposits imply larger volumes of transactions by depositors.[60]

For the period 1922–53 they plotted the ratios of member banks' net excess reserves to deposits against the Treasury bill rate in a scatter diagram, using annual data.[61] With interest rates on a logarithmic scale, they found that a good linear relationship could be fitted to the entire range of points. The years, 1920, 1921, 1931–33, and 1942–46, however, were disregarded in the fitting of the relationship. The fit was poor at the lower end, where interest rates were below 0.12 per cent, but in the higher ranges there was good agreement between experience of the late 1940's and early 1950's and that of the 1920's. Their conclusion was:

> The regression line based on this scatter of interest-reserve points indicates that a given proportional change in the short-term interest rate tends to affect the desired net excess reserves/deposit liabilities ratio by the same absolute amount, whatever the value of the initial interest rate.[62]

From this relationship, they said, the effect of a change in the interest rate on the banks' supply of deposits can be derived, and the effect of interest rate changes upon total money supply can be estimated, if the volume of currency in circulation is assumed to be proportional to deposits. They estimated that the banks' supply curve for money had a fairly constant elasticity, between 0.07 and 0.08 with respect to the interest rate.[63]

The Polak-White view of the role of member-bank reserve positions can be summed up about as follows: Assuming the total stock of member-bank reserves constant, an increase in the short-term interest rate induces banks to reduce the ratio of net excess reserves to total deposits, thus increasing total deposits. If the central bank changes the stock of reserves, changes in the short-term interest rate will still influence the volume of deposits through changing the ratio of total reserves to total deposits. Although Polak and White argue primarily in terms of changes in excess reserves, they could as well include changes in member-bank borrowings in their description of the interest-money supply relationship, since they use excess reserves minus borrowings in their regressions.

[60] *Ibid.*, p. 423.

[61] *Ibid.*, Chart 8, p. 424.

[62] *Ibid.*, p. 427.

[63] *Ibid.*, p. 428.

RECENT FREE-RESERVE THEORY

Although the concept of free reserves is used frequently in the financial press in discussion of monetary policy, the concept has had little attention in the economic journals. Federal Reserve publications have occasionally discussed the concept as an aid to understanding monetary policy, while emphasizing its limitations. A version of free reserve theory discussed by the Federal Reserve Bank of New York in 1958, for example, is evidently a lineal descendant of the Riefler-Burgess reserve position theory discussed earlier.[64] The one major change is the incorporation of excess reserves with member-bank borrowings. When free reserves of the member banks are high, according to the theory, market interest rates tend to fall and bank credit and the money supply tend to grow. When free reserves are low or negative, the converse is usually true: ". . . the result of sustained net borrowed reserves is restraint on bank credit, a lessened expansion (or possibly a moderate contraction) of the money supply, and a curbing of liquidity both within and outside the banking system."[65]

The 1961 edition of *The Federal Reserve System Purposes and Functions* stressed the need for observing net reserve positions of the member banks over a considerable period in attempting to discern changes in Federal Reserve policy:

Considering the complexity of the forces affecting the net reserve position in the short run—a fact reflected in the many sizable and irregular fluctuations in this measure from week to week—little or no significance can be attached to one week's shift. However, the trend in the net reserve figure, from sizable net borrowed reserves to small net free reserves over a period of several months preceding this particular week, clearly confirmed that Federal Reserve policy had been working to foster a larger flow of credit and money.[66]

The Federal Reserve Bank of New York similarly advised caution in interpreting the level of free reserves, saying: "Especially is it important to realize that a specific level of free reserves (negative or positive) may be associated with one degree of credit restraint or ease at one time, and with significantly different credit conditions in other periods."[67] The distribution of reserves among the banks, the strength of demand for credit, the relative proportions of various assets in bank portfolios, and the level and structure of interest rates were said to influence the significance of

[64] Federal Reserve Bank of New York, *Monthly Review*, November, 1958, pp. 162–67.

[65] *Ibid.*, p. 164.

[66] *The Federal Reserve System Purposes and Functions* (Fourth ed.; Washington, D.C.: Board of Governors of the Federal Reserve System, 1961), p. 211.

[67] Federal Reserve Bank of New York, *Monthly Review*, November, 1958, p. 164.

the free-reserve level. These qualifications are reminiscent of Currie's hypothesis that the sensitivity of banks to the level of their indebtedness varies from bank to bank and from time to time.

Although Federal Reserve publications acknowledge that System actions influence the free reserves, or net reserve positions, of member banks, they do not say that a precise control over reserve positions is either achieved or attempted.[68] According to *Purposes and Functions:*

While monetary policy necessarily influences the net reserve position of banks, this position in the short-run is also much affected by bank responses to the many cross currents that stem from the interplay of diverse market forces. For short-run interpretation, therefore, the net reserve position of the banking system may not always prove to be a reliable index of reserve banking policy. It is only one index of the direction of policy, and it is not always or necessarily the most important one.[69]

TOTAL RESERVES AND DEPOSIT EXPANSION

An argument for controlling deposit expansion through control of total reserves was stated long ago by W. F. Crick when he said, ". . . it is clear —or at least we must hope so—that the banks, so long as they maintain steady ratios of cash to deposits, are merely passive agents of Bank of England policy, as far as the volume of money in the form of credit is concerned."[70] A crucial question regarding his proposition is whether banks actually will maintain a steady ratio of cash to deposits or, in the American system, a steady ratio of bank reserves to deposits. Elsewhere in his study Crick made it clear that he did not expect the ratio to be absolutely constant but rather that banks will attempt to keep some desired ratio of cash assets to deposits. If a gain or loss of cash causes the actual ratio to be temporarily larger or smaller than the one the banks prefer, the banks

[68] Some outside observers believe, to the contrary, that net reserve positions actually are the principal day-to-day and week-to-week target of open-market operations. See in particular, Hobart C. Carr, "Why and How to Read the Federal Reserve Statement," *Journal of Finance*, XIV (December, 1959), 504–19; Colin D. Campbell, *The Federal Reserve and the Business Cycle* (Tuck Bulletin 26 [Hanover, New Hampshire: Amos Tuck School of Business Administration, 1961]); and Milton Friedman, *A Program for Monetary Stability* (New York: Fordham University Press, 1960), pp. 41–43. For other discussions bearing on free-reserve theory, see Ralph A. Young, "Tools and Processes of Monetary Policy," *United States Monetary Policy* (New York: American Assembly, 1958), pp. 35–36; Winfield W. Riefler, "Open Market Operations in Long-Term Securities," *Federal Reserve Bulletin*, XLIV, No. 11 (November, 1958), 1260–74; and Robert V. Roosa, "Credit Policy at the Discount Window: Comment," *Quarterly Journal of Economics*, LXXIII (May, 1959), 333–37.

[69] *Purposes and Functions*, p. 212.

[70] W. F. Crick, "The Genesis of Bank Deposits," *Economica*, VII (1927), 191–202, reprinted in *Readings in Monetary Theory* (New York: Blakiston Co., 1951), pp. 52–53.

will attempt to regain the desired ratio through buying or selling assets.

Much of the discussion of whether or not a central bank can control the money supply by controlling total reserves of the banks turns upon how much the ratio between reserves and deposits is likely to vary over time. Keynes, for example, thought reserve ratios in Great Britain and the United States were stable and that banks would seldom or never maintain idle reserves in excess of their conventional or legal proportion.[71] "Thus the facts show that, in the banking conditions which now exist in England and the United States," he said in 1930, "the aggregate of bank deposits . . . is a multiple, as nearly as possible constant, of the 'reserves' of the member banks."[72] A much different view was expressed a few years later by Lauchlin Currie:

> It may be justifiable for the purpose of exposition of principles to state, as is continually done, that an increase of $100 million in member bank reserves will, if utilized, result in an expansion of $1 billion in deposits. If, however, such a statement is meant to be an actual description of what happens, it is untrue. Actually an increase in utilized reserves may correspond with almost any multiple expansion or contraction of money.[73]

Among recent studies that have related quantities of reserves supplied to the banking system to changes in volume of earning assets or deposits of the banks are those of Robert P. Black, George Horwich, and Allan H. Meltzer.[74] Their studies tend to confirm the primacy of the central bank in the monetary system, with each of them focusing on a different aspect of the problem. Black was concerned with the responses of banks to large discrete injections of reserves produced by reserve requirement reductions; Horwich measured the speed and magnitude with which banks change their holdings of earning assets in response to changes in reserve holdings; and Meltzer demonstrated that a close and stable relationship existed between the money supply of France and the monetary liabilities of the central bank despite the disturbances of war, occupation, and reconstruction.

[71] Keynes, *A Treatise on Money*, II, 53–66.

[72] *Ibid.*, p. 64.

[73] Currie, *The Supply and Control of Money*, p. 82. See also pp. 69–82, 163–79.

[74] Robert P. Black, "An Analysis of the Impacts of the 1953 and 1954 Reductions in Federal Reserve Member Bank Reserve Requirements" (Ph.D. diss., Graduate Faculty of the University of Virginia, 1955); George Horwich, "Elements of Timing and Response in the Balance Sheet of Banking, 1953–55," *Journal of Finance*, XII (May, 1957), 238–55; Allan H. Meltzer, "The Behavior of the French Money Supply: 1938–54," *Journal of Political Economy*, LXVII (June, 1959), 275–96. Another study bearing on the reserve ratio is by Stephen L. McDonald, "The Internal Drain and Bank Credit Expansion," *Journal of Finance*, VIII (December, 1953), 407–21.

Black's objectives were to examine the effectiveness of reserve requirement changes as instruments of monetary policy; to estimate the reserve-deposit multiplier; and to measure the time required for all of the effects of a reserve injection to be produced. In a sense his model could be interpreted in terms of actual and desired reserve positions. Starting from an initial position of equilibrium with excess reserves at the level desired by banks, the banks suddenly experience a large increase in their excess reserves. The questions concerning Black then were: Do the banks return actual excess reserves to the initially desired level? How long does the adjustment process take?

Black discovered in the particular episodes he examined that the banks actually used more reserves in the expansion following each reserve requirement reduction than were freed by the reduction.[75] He concluded that apparently banks watch their reserve accounts closely enough that reserves will not lie idle if loan or investment outlets are readily available. He also discovered that the adjustment process was prompt; the expansion of deposits reached almost its full limit within one reserve period following each reduction in requirements. He pointed out that the marginal rates of change of some of the variables in his expansion equations were unstable, making short-run prediction of the effects of reserve requirement reductions difficult. However, he believed that the behavior of these variables would be much more stable over longer periods of time. Thus, changes in reserve requirements, and presumably other changes in member-bank reserves as well, should have predictable effects over the long run.

George Horwich concluded that the response of bankers to changes in effective reserves usually occurred in an interval of less than a month.[76] He also found that occasionally responses appropriate to one month or a series of months were carried over to one or two months in which they were not appropriate.[77] The linear correlation coefficient between monthly increments of effective reserves and of earning assets was 0.59, and there were occasional months in which the directions of movement of the two

---

[75] Black, "Impacts of 1953 and 1954 Reductions of Member Bank Reserve Requirements," pp. 269–87.

[76] Horwich, *Journal of Finance*, XII (May, 1957), 254. His concept of "effective reserves" means reserves adjusted to take account of the varying availability of reserves and adjusted to express reserves of comparable availability in terms of a constant reserve requirement. In this paper, rates of change of total reserves and unborrowed reserves were adjusted for changes in reserve requirements but not for the other factors taken into account by Horwich. See chap. iii, below, and Horwich, pp. 238–47 and 255.

[77] *Ibid.*, p. 252.

were not the same.[78] His findings in this regard are thus consistent with characteristic lags in the mechanism described later in this study. Fluctuation in his series of effective reserves was greater than the fluctuation in earning assets, in relative terms, indicating that changes in excess reserves tend to damp the asset-change response of banks to changes in reserves in the short run. He observed also that reserves appeared to be used more intensively when interest rates were rising than when rates were falling, but he did not not attempt to establish a causal relationship.[79] Horwich's results thus confirm the ability of the central bank to influence banks' holdings of earning assets or deposits over time but do not indicate that the change in assets for a particular month can be predicted with much precision from the change in effective reserves.

Meltzer's objective was to analyze the behavior of the money supply in an economy undergoing inflation. He found that the monetary base could be used to predict the money supply with an average error of less than $1\frac{1}{2}$ per cent. He concluded:

The data indicate that the coefficient of multiple expansion was largely unaffected by changes in social institutions but was markedly affected by particular monetary policies. This result and our ability to predict changes in the money supply indicate that the central bank—though legally empowered to control the money issue through open-market operations, rediscount rate changes, and a variety of postwar direct controls over banks—was primarily responsible for the increase in the money supply.[80]

One of the most interesting parts of his study, for its contrast to the American practice of considering legal reserve requirements as an essential fulcrum for central-bank influence, was his demonstration of the close relationship between the cash assets and the demand deposits of the commercial banks. His underlying assumption was that cash assets are held as precautionary reserves against various forms of drain in a banking system without legal reserves. "Given the distribution of deposits, the amount of precautionary reserves held is based on a probability distribution for the expected drain. All reserves above the amount required on the basis of this probability distribution are excess reserves."[81] In a footnote he applied his "reserve policy" equation to a system in which there are legal reserves.

[78] For January, 1947, through December, 1958, the coefficient of simple correlation between the monthly per cent change in total reserves adjusted for changes in reserve requirements and the monthly per cent change in total member-bank deposits subject to reserve requirements found in this study was 0.88.

[79] *Ibid.*, pp. 251–52.

[80] Meltzer, *Journal of Political Economy*, LXVII (June, 1959), 288.

[81] *Ibid.*, pp. 278–79.

There are then three types of reserves, which can be designated as legal, precautionary, and excess reserves. The legal reserves are in a sense frozen. In addition to them, the banker must maintain a precautionary reserve corresponding in principle to the precautionary reserve of a banker in a system without legal reserves. From this view there is little or no difference; Q, in equation (5) can represent legal and precautionary reserves or simply precautionary reserves.[82]

Edward C. Simmons, on the other hand, has stressed the instability of the relationship between member-bank reserves and deposits or money supply, considering instability to be an inherent characteristic of a fractional reserve banking system composed of a large number of banks. In a review of monetary developments in the immediate postwar years he concluded that "efforts to employ monetary policy as a stabilizer may be thwarted by the tendency of the system to produce autonomous changes in the money supply."[83] In each of six half-year intervals he cited as examples, changes in total member-bank reserves and changes in adjusted demand deposits of all commercial banks were consistently in the same direction, but their rates of change did not correspond. One of the sources of instability he emphasized in the article was variation in the average reserve requirement ratio caused by shifting of deposits among banks subject to different reserve requirements.[84] He also cited what he characterized as exceptionally severe short-run fluctuations in member-bank reserves in the early postwar period that presented difficult adjustment problems for the banks.[85]

The studies cited above suggest that banks respond with alacrity to changes in their stock of reserves so that the central bank should be able to control total deposits or money supply effectively by controlling total reserves. The degree of precision with which control can be effected has not been clearly established, however. Some economists, such as Lauchlin Currie and Edward C. Simmons, have argued that changes in the rela-

---

[82] Meltzer, *ibid.*, fn. 8, p. 278. The equation (5) referred to is:

$$Q = Q(D_{cb}^{p})$$

in which Q = cash assets of commercial banks and D_{cb}^{p} = deposits of the public in commercial banks. An alternative form of the equation is:

$$Q = q(D_{cb}^{p}, T_{cb} + T_{ce})$$

in which T_{cb} = time deposits at commercial banks and T_{ce} = savings deposits at commercial banks.

[83] Simmons, *Journal of Political Economy*, LVIII (April, 1950), 124.

[84] *Ibid.*, pp. 127–34.

[85] *Ibid.*, pp. 134–41.

tionship between member-bank reserves and deposits or money supply may present an almost insuperable obstacle to Federal Reserve efforts to control the money supply unless the system is overhauled.[86] Others, such as George Tolley and Milton Friedman, have argued that although variations in ratios of reserves to deposits or money supply occur they could be offset with open-market operations in order to produce any desired money supply.[87]

THE EXCESS RESERVES OF THE 1930'S

The growth of excess reserves between 1932 and 1942 has often been cited as evidence of the ineffectiveness of open-market operations in some circumstances. The Federal Reserve System, following reserve position doctrine, believed that the excess reserves would make it difficult for open-market operations to compel banks to borrow and thereby to restrain credit expansion. Fortunately, restraint was not deemed necessary in those years, however. The System portfolio was kept constant in amount from the fall of 1933 till August, 1939, except for relatively minor purchases in 1937. An inflow of gold from abroad was considered to be the principal reason for the growth of excess reserves. Reserve requirements were doubled in two steps in 1936 and 1937 in order to reduce the excess reserves. It was not expected that the change in reserve requirements would have any immediate influence on bank credit expansion; the action was said to be a precautionary measure to prevent an uncontrollable expansion of credit in the future. As a substitute for the conventional methods of control, emphasis in open-market operations was shifted from influencing member-bank reserves to influencing conditions in the capital markets in 1939.[88]

Although the Federal Reserve was most concerned about growth of excess reserves as a hindrance to possible efforts to restrain credit expansion, the experience of the 1930's has been put forward also as evidence that growth of excess reserves may limit the power of open-market operations to induce credit expansion. According to the liquidity trap hypothesis, if interest rates are low banks may be unwilling to expand loans and investments when provided with additional reserves unless there is an

---

[86] Currie, *The Supply and Control of Money*, pp. 69–82; and Edward C. Simmons, "The Monetary Mechanism Since the War," *Journal of Political Economy*, LVII (April, 1950), 124–41.

[87] George S. Tolley, "Providing for Growth of the Money Supply," *Journal of Political Economy*, LXV (December, 1957), 465–85; and Milton Friedman, *A Program for Monetary Stability*, pp. 30–35.

[88] See, *Annual Reports of the Board of Governors of the Federal Reserve System*, for 1937, pp. 2–15; 1938, pp. 4–6, 18–29; 1939, pp. 2–14.

increase in the demand for credit. Furthermore, some of the banks' excess reserves could be taken away from them without affecting the volume of bank credit. This was apparently the opinion of the Federal Reserve at the time of the 1936 and 1937 reserve requirement increases. George R. Morrison has suggested an alternative hypothesis: The banking panic, changes in default experience on loans, and changes in reserve-requirement regulations, increased the banks' estimates of the volume of excess reserves they needed to hold for their own protection during the 1930's. Even though excess reserves were large by historical standards, they were not necessarily greater than the banks wanted them to be, according to his hypothesis. Open-market operations of the Federal Reserve, therefore, actually might have been able to influence the banks to expand or to contract credit and deposits.[89] The sharp contraction of deposits following the 1936 and 1937 increases in reserve requirements tends to support his interpretation.[90]

SOME CONCLUSIONS FROM THE LITERATURE

Some of the writers discussed in this chapter have submitted evidence that open-market operations can control the rate of deposit expansion by controlling total reserves. Their conclusion, however, has been questioned on two general grounds:

1. The ratio of reserves to deposits may be so variable that the central bank cannot predict the results of its efforts to change deposits through changing the volume of reserves.

2. The central bank may not have effective control of total reserves, in the American system, because the banks may offset open-market operations with changes in the volume of their borrowings.

The development of reserve position doctrine can be attributed at least partly to the second objection to control through total reserves. Reserve position doctrine, in turn, is subject to the following objections:

1. The Federal Reserve may not be able to control the volume of member-bank borrowings or free reserves.

2. The level of member-bank borrowings or free reserves in turn may not be predictably related to the rate of bank-credit expansion.

Without settling these issues, the literature surveyed has indicated that bank behavior is influenced by Federal Reserve open-market opera-

[89] George R. Morrison, "Portfolio Behavior of Banks" (draft report, Federal Reserve Bank of St. Louis, September, 1960), pp. 24–33.

[90] For some arguments supporting the liquidity-trap hypothesis, see John H. Kareken, "Our Knowledge of Monetary Policy," *American Economic Review*, LI, No. 2 (May, 1961), 41–44.

tions, the market factors affecting the supply of reserves, the level of member-bank borrowing, the level of excess reserves, market interest rates, the discount rate, bankers' reluctance to borrow, the demand for bank credit, and bankers' expectations of various sorts. Disputes over the central bank's ability to control the money supply and over the choice of methods reduce largely to differences in the relative weights assigned to these variables. Furthermore, both main schools in the controversy traced here have contributed useful insights regarding behavior of the monetary system.

III

The Accounting Framework and Some Preliminary Observations on Member-Bank Behavior

DERIVATION OF SOME USEFUL ACCOUNTING IDENTITIES

IN ORDER to narrow the problem, it will be helpful to express some of the characteristics of the monetary system in a set of identities. Let

M be the money supply of the United States, defined as currency in circulation plus demand deposits in commercial banks plus time deposits in commercial banks;[1]

C be currency in circulation;[2]

$\dfrac{C}{M}$ be the ratio of currency in circulation to total money supply;

D_S be demand and time deposits of member banks of the Federal Reserve System;

$\dfrac{D_S}{M}$ be the ratio of member-bank deposits to total money supply;

D_N be demand and time deposits of nonmember banks; and

$\dfrac{D_N}{M}$ be the ratio of deposits in nonmember banks to total money supply.

The rate of change of total money supply in relative terms then is

$$\frac{1}{M}\frac{dM}{dt} = \frac{C}{M}\cdot\frac{1}{C}\frac{dC}{dt} + \frac{D_S}{M}\cdot\frac{1}{D_S}\frac{dD}{dt} + \frac{D_N}{M}\cdot\frac{1}{D_N}\frac{dD_N}{dt}. \quad (3.1)$$

The part of identity (3.1) selected for attention in this study is the rate of change of member-bank deposits, $(1/D_S)(dD_S/dt)$, which in turn can

---

[1] This definition of money supply differs from most in that Treasury balances in commercial banks are not excluded. The Treasury balances are included primarily for reasons of convenience in using net member-bank demand deposits subject to reserve requirements, which include Treasury balances. Adjustment to the conventional concept of privately held money supply was not considered necessary for the purposes of this study.

[2] Currency in circulation is defined as currency outside the Treasury, Federal Reserve Banks, and the commercial banks.

be related to changes in reserves in another identity derived from the accounting relationships of a fractional reserve banking system. Let

D_S be total member-bank deposits (the subscript S will be omitted henceforward);

R_R be total member-bank required reserves;

$\dfrac{R_R}{D} = y$ be the reserve requirement ratio;

R_E be excess reserves of the member banks;

$\dfrac{R_E}{D} = x$ be the excess reserve ratio, or voluntary reserve ratio;

R be total reserves of the member banks at Federal Reserve Banks;

$\dfrac{R}{D} = x + y = z$ be the total reserve ratio.

Then,

$$D = \frac{R}{z}, \tag{3.2}$$

$$\log D = \log R - \log z. \tag{3.3}$$

Differentiating (3.3) with respect to time,

$$\frac{1}{D}\frac{dD}{dt} = \frac{1}{R}\frac{dR}{dt} - \frac{1}{z}\frac{dz}{dt}. \tag{3.4}$$

From equation (3.4) it can be seen that the percentage rate of change in total member-bank deposits will be equal to the rate of change of total reserves if the total reserve ratio, z, is constant; the rate of change of deposits will be smaller than the rate of change of reserves if the reserve ratio is increasing; and the rate of change of deposits will be greater than the rate of change of reserves if the reserve ratio is decreasing. An increase of the reserve ratio absorbs reserves that otherwise would have supported deposit expansion; a decrease releases reserves.

Equation (3.4) can also be expressed as

$$\frac{1}{D}\frac{dD}{dt} = \frac{1}{R}\frac{dR}{dt} - \frac{D}{R}\frac{d(R/D)}{dt}. \tag{3.5}$$

The rates of change of the required reserve ratio and the excess reserve ratio can be distinguished.

$$\frac{1}{D}\frac{dD}{dt} = \frac{1}{R}\frac{dR}{dt} - \frac{D}{R}\frac{d(R_R/D)}{dt} - \frac{D}{R}\frac{d(R_E/D)}{dt}. \tag{3.6}$$

If equation (3.6) is expressed in absolute terms it becomes

$$\frac{dD}{dt} = \frac{D}{R}\frac{dR}{dt} - \frac{D^2}{R}\frac{d(R_R/D)}{dt} - \frac{D^2}{R}\frac{d(R_E/D)}{dt}. \qquad (3.7)$$

Equation (3.7) is a general statement of the familiar multiple-expansion principle. The potential rate of expansion of deposits resulting from a given rate of change of total reserves, if expressed in its most simple form in the notation employed here, would be

$$\frac{dD}{dt} = \frac{D}{R_R}\frac{dR}{dt}. \qquad (3.8)$$

Equation (3.8) implies that the reserve requirement ratio and the volume of excess reserves are constant.[3] Equation (3.7), on the other hand, makes allowances for changes in the reserve requirement ratio and in excess reserves.

Equation (3.6) accounts for the allocation of reserves between excess and required reserves without distinguishing among sources of changes in the total stock of reserves. To distinguish the various sources, let

$\dfrac{dG}{dt}$ be the rate of gold inflow;

$\dfrac{dC}{dt}$ be the rate of increase of currency in circulation;

$\dfrac{dC_V}{dt}$ be the rate of increase of member-bank vault cash, other than cash allowable as reserves;[4]

---

[3] The multiplier conventionally used, however, often includes other items such as excess reserves and currency; for example, Albert G. Hart, *Money, Debt, and Economic Activity* (2d ed.; New York: Prentice-Hall, Inc., 1953), pp. 76–77.

[4] Beginning in December, 1959, a portion of member-bank vault cash could be included as part of the legal reserves of the member banks. In Federal Reserve System accounting for the factors affecting reserves before that date, member-bank vault cash (other than the portion eligible as reserves) was included with currency held by the public, and no distinction was made between them. Thus, a given change in currency in circulation, as defined by the Federal Reserve for reserve accounting purposes, might be brought about by a change in the public's holdings of currency, by a change in member-bank vault cash, or by some combination of the two. In the empirical work of this study the Federal Reserve convention has been followed; the aggregate reserves data are for member-bank reserve balances at the Federal Reserve Banks, and changes in member-bank vault cash are among the factors affecting the reserve balances, although they are not specifically identified. Before November, 1958, there were no daily-average data on member-bank vault cash comparable to the other daily-average reserve data so it would not have been practicable to distinguish changes in vault cash in the factors affecting reserves. Begin-

$\dfrac{dF}{dt}$ be the rate of increase in Federal Reserve float;

$\dfrac{dT}{dt}$ be the rate of increase of Treasury cash and Treasury balances at the Federal Reserve Banks;

$\dfrac{dO}{dt}$ be the rate of increase of foreign and other deposits at Federal Reserve Banks, and of other Federal Reserve accounts;[5]

$\dfrac{dP}{dt}$ be the rate of Federal Reserve open-market purchases (net of sales);

$\dfrac{dR_B}{dt}$ be the rate of increase of member-bank borrowing from the Federal Reserve.

Then

$$\frac{dR}{dt} = \frac{dG}{dt} - \frac{dC}{dt} - \frac{dC_V}{dt} + \frac{dF}{dt} - \frac{dT}{dt} - \frac{dO}{dt} + \frac{dP}{dt} + \frac{dR_B}{dt}. \quad (3.9)$$

The market factors in equation (3.9) can be summed with the rate of open-market purchases of the Federal Reserve to obtain a net rate of change of unborrowed reserves, dR_U/dt. Because the Federal Reserve can in principle offset with open-market operations the flows of reserves from the other sources, dR_U/dt can be considered to be the net rate at which reserves are added to the banking system at the volition of the Federal Reserve, or the rate at which the Federal Reserve permits the banks to acquire reserves from all sources other than borrowing. Equation (3.9) then becomes

$$\frac{dR}{dt} = \frac{dR_U}{dt} + \frac{dR_B}{dt}, \quad (3.10)$$

$$R_U = R - R_B, \quad (3.11)$$

and

$$R_U = R_E + R_R - R_B. \quad (3.12)$$

---

ning in November, 1958, however, member banks have been required to report their daily holdings of vault cash so in future studies it will be possible to isolate changes in vault cash. Theoretical implications of the treatment of vault cash described here will be discussed in chapter iv.

[5] The other deposits referred to are deposits at Federal Reserve Banks other than member-bank reserve balances and Treasury balances. The other accounts include capital and surplus accounts of the Federal Reserve Banks and miscellaneous other liabilities. They do not include deferred availability cash items, which are reflected in float. Federal Reserve note liabilities are reflected in currency in circulation.

Let

$$\frac{R_B}{D} = w \qquad \text{be the ratio of borrowings to total deposits; and}$$

$$\frac{R_U}{D} = x + y - w = v \qquad \text{be the ratio of unborrowed reserves to total deposits.}$$

Then,

$$D = \frac{R_U}{v}, \tag{3.13}$$

$$\frac{1}{D}\frac{dD}{dt} = \frac{1}{R_U}\frac{dR_U}{dt} - \frac{1}{v}\frac{dv}{dt}, \tag{3.14}$$

$$\frac{1}{D}\frac{dD}{dt} = \frac{1}{R_U}\frac{dR_U}{dt} - \frac{D}{R_U}\frac{d(R_R/D)}{dt} - \frac{D}{R_U}\frac{d(R_E/D)}{dt}$$
$$+ \frac{D}{R_U}\frac{d(R_B/D)}{dt}. \tag{3.15}$$

The identity expressed in (3.15) arranges in a convenient form four variables that influence the rate of change of deposits.

$\dfrac{dR_U}{dt}$ is the rate of change of unborrowed reserves per unit of time;

$\dfrac{d(R_R/D)}{dt}$ is the rate of change of the reserve-requirement ratio;

$\dfrac{d(R_E/D)}{dt}$ is the rate of change of the excess reserve ratio; and

$\dfrac{d(R_B/D)}{dt}$ is the rate of change of the ratio of borrowings to total deposits.

If excess reserves and borrowings are combined in free reserves the identity (3.15) becomes

$$\frac{1}{D}\frac{dD}{dt} = \frac{1}{R_U}\frac{dR_U}{dt} - \frac{D}{R_U}\frac{d(R_R/D)}{dt} - \frac{D}{R_U}\frac{d(R_F/D)}{at}. \tag{3.16}$$

Free reserves are used in much of the following discussion rather than the component excess reserves and borrowings, in part for convenience in exposition and in part because there are plausible theoretical grounds for this procedure. The question whether excess reserves and borrowings should be treated separately or as combined in free reserves will be kept open, however, for empirical examination.

SOME PRELIMINARY OBSERVATIONS OF MEMBER-BANK BEHAVIOR

An appreciation of the relative influence of the variables in equations (3.15) and (3.16) can be gained from Figures 1, 3, and 4. The dotted line in Figure 1 represents the monthly rate of change in unborrowed reserves, $(1/R_U)(dR_U/dt)$, for the years 1947–58. The solid line is the rate of change of total deposits. The striking feature of this chart is the wide divergence

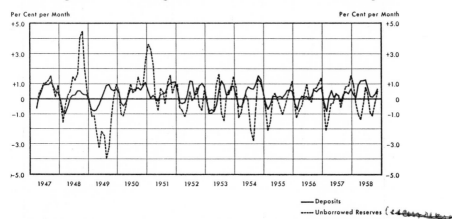

FIG. 1.—Rates of change of total member-bank unborrowed reserves and total member-bank deposits subject to reserve requirements, February, 1947, through November, 1958. Reserves and deposits data are monthly averages of daily figures. Rates of change are calculated from changes in monthly averages from midmonth to midmonth and are expressed in terms of per cent per month. The rates of change have been smoothed with a three-month weighted moving average with weights of $\frac{1}{4}$ on the first month, $\frac{1}{2}$ on the center month, and $\frac{1}{4}$ on the third month. Demand deposits subject to reserve requirements are total demand deposits minus cash items in process of collection and demand balances due from domestic banks (also minus war loan and Series E bond accounts until June 30, 1947). All time deposits are subject to reserve requirements.

Source: J.1 Releases of the Board of Governors of the Federal Reserve System: "Deposits, Reserves, and Borrowings of Member Banks."

between the rates of change of unborrowed reserves and deposits, a divergence attributable to the remaining three variables in equation (3.15). If the reserve requirement ratio, the excess reserve ratio, and the ratio of borrowings to deposits had remained constant the two lines would have coincided.

The behavior of the reserve requirement ratio from 1947 through 1958 is illustrated in Figure 2, in which the solid line is average reserve requirement ratio, R_R/D. Changes of reserve requirements by the Board of Governors produced the major shifts in the ratio, but shifts in the distribution

of deposits among the various classes of banks and in the relative proportions of time and demand deposits in the total have also caused changes
in the ratio.[6] Between early 1955 and the end of 1957, for example, the
reserve-requirement ratio drifted lower, thereby releasing reserves to
support deposit expansion.[7]

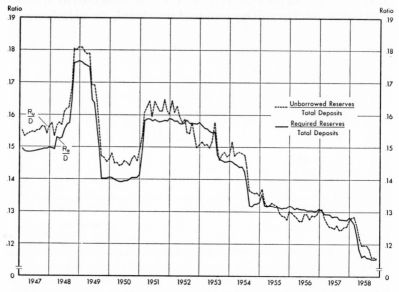

FIG. 2.—Member-bank reserve-deposit ratios, January, 1947–December,
1958, inclusive. Monthly averages of daily total member-bank unborrowed reserves and of total required reserves have been divided by monthly averages
of total daily member-bank deposits subject to reserve requirements to obtain
the ratios plotted.

Source: J.1 Releases of the Board of Governors of the Federal Reserve System: "Deposits, Reserves, and Borrowings of Member Banks."

[6] Currie stressed such changes in reserve requirements as a source of autonomous
changes in money supply; Currie, *Supply and Control of Money*, pp. 69–82. See also
Tinbergen, *Business Cycles in the United States*, pp. 87–88; George Horwich, "Elements
of Timing and Response in the Balance Sheet of Banking," *Journal of Finance*, XII
(May, 1957), 238–39; George S. Tolley, "Providing for Growth of the Money Supply,"
Journal of Political Economy, LXV (December, 1957), 466–73, 484–85; Clark Warburton, "Bank Reserves and Business Fluctuations," *Journal of the American Statistical
Association*, XLIII (December, 1948), 547–58; and Edward C. Simmons, "The Monetary Mechanism since the War," *Journal of Political Economy*, LVIII, No. 2 (April,
1950), 124–33.

[7] Time deposits grew in relation to demand deposits from 1955 through the middle of
1958, and the share of central reserve city banks in total member-bank deposits declined
over the same period. Both of these shifts tended to reduce the average reserve requirement ratio for all member banks.

In Figure 3 the rate of change of unborrowed reserves has been adjusted for changes in the reserve-requirement ratio by subtracting the relative rate of change of the reserve-requirement ratio, $(D/R_U)(d[R_R/D]/dt)$ from $(1/R_U)(dR_U/dt)$, the rate of change of unborrowed reserves. It would appear from comparison of Figures 1 and 3 that a large part of

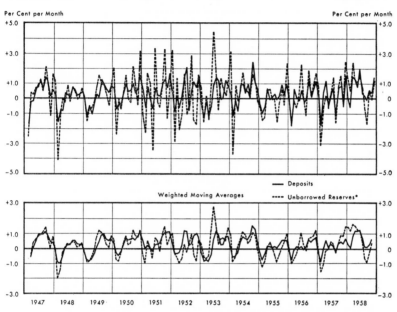

Fig. 3.—Rates of change of total member-bank deposits subject to reserve requirements and of total unborrowed reserves adjusted for changes in average reserve-requirement ratio, January, 1947, through December, 1958. Rates of change in the lower panel have been smoothed with a three-month weighted moving average with weights of $\frac{1}{4}$, $\frac{1}{2}$, $\frac{1}{4}$. Rates of change have been calculated from the changes in monthly averages of daily reserves and deposits, centered at midmonths and are expressed in per cent per month. Adjustment for changes in the reserve-requirement ratio has been made by subtracting the relative change in the reserve-requirement ratio each month from the percentage change in unborrowed reserves, according to the formula:

$$\left(\frac{1}{R_U}\frac{dR_U}{dt}\right)^* = \frac{1}{R_U}\frac{dR_U}{dt} - \frac{D}{R_U}\frac{d(R_R/D)}{dt}.$$

The asterisk denotes the adjusted rate of change of unborrowed reserves. See discussion on pages 32–36 for definitions of the symbols and for derivation of the formula. See notes to Figure 1 for definition of deposits subject to reserve requirements.

Source: J.1 Releases of the Board of Governors of the Federal Reserve System: "Deposits, Reserves, and Borrowings of Member Banks."

the variation in the rate of change of deposits can be accounted for by variation in the rate of change of unborrowed reserves and in the reserve-requirement ratio. Furthermore, it would appear that the residual variation, which is the subject of this study, behaves in a systematic manner.

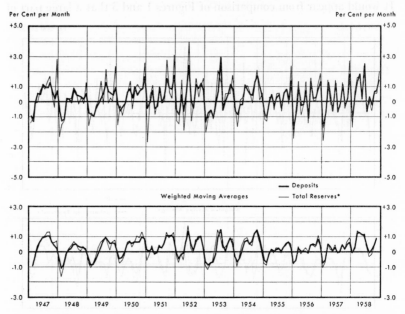

Fig. 4.—Rates of change of total member-bank deposits subject to reserve requirements and of total reserves adjusted for changes in the average reserve-requirement ratio, January, 1947, through December, 1958. Rates of change in the lower panel have been smoothed with a three-month weighted moving average with weights of $\frac{1}{4}, \frac{1}{2}, \frac{1}{4}$. All rates of change have been calculated from changes in monthly averages of daily deposits and reserves centered on ends of months, so that the rate of change for a month is the rate at which deposits or reserves changed during the month, rather than the rate of change during the period from the middle of the month to the next month, as in Figures 1 and 3. The rate of change of total reserves has been adjusted for changes in the reserve requirement ratio according to the formula:

$$\left(\frac{1}{R}\frac{dR}{dt}\right)^* = \frac{1}{R}\frac{dR}{dt} - \frac{D}{R}\frac{d(R_R/D)}{dt}.$$

The asterisk denotes the adjusted rate of change of total reserves. See discussion on pages 32–36 for definitions of the symbols and for derivation of the formula. See notes to Figure 1 for definition of deposits subject to reserve requirements.

Source: J.1 Releases of the Board of Governors of the Federal Reserve System: "Deposits, Reserves, and Borrowings of Member Banks."

The rates of change of unborrowed reserves and of the required reserves ratio are considered to be autonomously determined for the purposes of this study, although their behavior presents interesting questions for investigation.

The influence of changes in the free-reserve ratio (or in the excess reserves and borrowings ratios) is illustrated clearly in Figure 3 by the experience of 1957 and 1958. In the first third of 1957 the rate of change of deposits was greater than the rate at which unborrowed reserves changed (after adjustment for changes in the reserve-requirement ratio). In other words, while reserves were being withdrawn by the Federal Reserve during most of this period, deposits either contracted more slowly than unborrowed reserves or actually expanded. Part of the effect of the reduction in reserves was evidently offset by a decline of the free-reserve ratio. From October, 1957, until May, 1958, on the other hand, the rate of growth of deposits was considerably smaller than the rate of growth of unborrowed reserves. During this period the free-reserve ratio rose, as some of the additional reserves provided by the Federal Reserve were used by the banks to increase excess reserves and/or to pay off borrowings at the Federal Reserve. The free-reserve ratio declined again after June, 1958. Deposits kept growing, although at a slower rate, despite the fact that total unborrowed reserves declined for several months.

In Figure 4, rates of change of total reserves adjusted for reserve-requirement changes are plotted with rates of change of total deposits subject to reserve requirements. Any divergence between the two lines is attributable to changes in the ratio of excess reserves to deposits. One interesting feature of this chart is that the rates of change of reserves and deposits agree more closely in the later years of the period covered, say from about 1954 on, than in the earlier years. This suggests that the speed of adjustment of the banks to changes in the stock of reserves increased.

IV

Development of the Hypotheses

INTRODUCTION

THE PROBLEM of this chapter is to develop a theory or hypothesis by which the behavior of the excess reserves ratio and the borrowings ratio, R_E/D and R_B/D, may be explained. The theory should be able to predict under specified conditions the values of these ratios and their rates of change per unit of time. The hypothesis is developed here for their behavior as combined in the free-reserve ratio, R_F/D. Theoretical implications of treating them separately or in combined form are discussed later in the chapter.

In order to concentrate attention upon open-market operations of the Federal Reserve, market interest rates, and the discount rate, the hypotheses will be stated in the form of a description of a banking and monetary system that has been stripped of all but the most essential features. Many interesting details of actual behavior of the United States monetary system must be excluded for the sake of simplicity. Whether or not the explanation has been oversimplified or whether additional influences should have been considered will be examined when the hypotheses are subjected to empirical testing in chapter v.

BEHAVIOR OF INDIVIDUAL BANKS

The first assumption is that each bank attempts to maintain some desired free-reserve position to provide for expected and unexpected clearings drains and that this desired reserve position is related to total deposits, market interest rates, and the discount rate. Free reserves of the individual bank are defined as excess reserves at the Federal Reserve, balances with other member banks, and loans to other member banks, minus borrowings from the Federal Reserve, balances due to other member banks, and borrowings from other member banks.[1]

Let

R'_{Fi} be desired free reserves of bank i;

D_i be total deposits of bank i;

r_m be market interest rates; and

r_d be the Federal Reserve discount rate

$$R'_{Fi} = f(D_i, r_m, r_d) . \qquad (4.1)$$

[1] Transactions with non-member banks are treated here as transactions with the non-bank public.

Desired free reserves might instead be related to demand deposits and time deposits on the assumption that bank expectations of drains from the two types of deposits are different. Using D_{Ti} for time deposits of bank i and D_{Di} for demand deposits of bank i,

$$R'_{Fi} = f(D_{Ti}, D_{Di}, r_m, r_d) . \qquad (4.2)$$

The simpler assumption of equation (4.1) is the one used here, however.[2]

It is further assumed that the relationship represented by equation (4.1) is homogeneous of degree 1 in D. Therefore, if $(R_F/D)'_i$ is the desired free-reserve ratio,

$$\left(\frac{R_F}{D}\right)'_i = g(r_m, r_d) . \qquad (4.3)$$

Let

R_{Fi} be actual free reserves of bank i;

R_{Ei} be excess reserves of bank i at the Federal Reserve;

D_{Fi} be balances due from other member banks (interbank deposits);

R_{Li} be reserves loaned to other banks (Federal funds);

R_{BFi} be reserves borrowed from the Federal Reserve;

D_{Bi} be balances due to other member banks;

R_{BBi} be reserves borrowed from other member banks.

Then,

$$R_{Fi} = R_{Ei} + D_{Fi} + R_{Li} - R_{BFi} - D_{Bi} - R_{BBi} . \qquad (4.4)$$

To meet a clearings drain a bank can draw upon any one or a combination of the sources in equation (4.4), all of which provide immediately available reserve funds. As the bank gains or loses reserves through clearings, the actual ratio of its free reserves to deposits, $(R_F/D)_i$, may depart from the desired ratio, $(R_F/D)'_i$, inducing the bank to adjust by selling earning assets or buying assets (or making loans).

The greater the difference between the actual and desired free-reserve ratios, the greater is the rate at which the bank attempts to change the actual ratio. Another major assumption about individual bank behavior, therefore, is the adjustment function, equation (4.5), which relates the

---

[2] See Meltzer's discussion of precautionary reserves, *Journal of Political Economy*, LXVII (June, 1959), 278–80. For another discussion of uncertainty and the management of a bank's reserve position, see Daniel Orr and W. G. Melton, "Stochastic Reserve Losses and Expansion of Bank Credit," *American Economic Review*, LI (September, 1961), 614–23.

bank's desired rate of change of the free-reserve ratio to the difference between the actual and the desired ratios.

$$\left[\frac{d(R_F/D)}{dt}\right]_i' = f\left[\left(\frac{R_F}{D}\right)_i' - \left(\frac{R_F}{D}\right)_i\right]. \tag{4.5}$$

BEHAVIOR OF THE SYSTEM

When the free reserves of the individual banks—equation (4.4)—are aggregated for all member banks, the intermember-bank balances and the intermember-bank loans cancel out, leaving free reserves for the system consisting of total excess reserves at the Federal Reserve minus total borrowings from the Federal Reserve:

$$R_F = R_E - R_B. \tag{4.6}$$

Summing the desired reserve ratios of the individual banks implies some desired ratio of free reserves to deposits for the system as a whole. The actual reserve ratio may depart from the desired in a particular time period as actual free reserves of the member banks are influenced by flows of reserves into and out of the system. When the actual free-reserve ratio differs from the desired ratio, the banks can attempt to adjust by expanding or contracting loans and investments, thus changing required reserves and total deposits, or by borrowing from the Federal Reserve. For example, when the actual ratio of free reserves to deposits exceeds the desired ratio banks expand loans and investments, causing required reserves and deposits to rise. The individual bank can change its free-reserve ratio by selling earning assets to another bank or lending reserves to other banks. But the free-reserve ratio for the banking system as a whole can be changed only through transactions with the non-bank public or the Federal Reserve.

THE TREATMENT OF VAULT CASH

It might be expected that member-bank vault cash would be included with other reserve items influencing bank behavior, yet in this study it has been excluded. There are several reasons for this treatment. In the first place, one of the objectives of the study was to examine the free-reserve concept used in the Federal Reserve System and by others for many years, a concept which has not included vault cash. Therefore, the hypotheses of this study were framed in terms of the concept as conventionally defined. In further work on the other main objective of the study —to develop a theory of money-supply determination—experiments should be made with vault cash included in free reserves, or excess reserves, to determine whether better predictions of the rate of change of deposits or money supply could be obtained in that way. As was explained in chapter iii above, comparable daily-average data for member-bank vault cash were not available, however, before November, 1958.[3]

A second major argument for excluding vault cash from reserves at this stage of the inquiry is a hypothesis that the banks' demand function for vault cash is significantly different from the demand function for reserves defined as balances at the Federal Reserve Banks minus borrowings from the Federal Reserve. An alternative formulation of the accounting identity (3.16) from chapter iii should make more clear the organization of topics for investigation envisioned here. If total member-bank reserves are defined as excess reserves at the Federal Reserve Banks plus required reserves at the Federal Reserve Banks[4] plus the portion of vault cash not permitted to be included in legal reserves and if changes in vault cash are not included in the factors affecting reserves,[5] equation (3.16) would become:

$$\frac{1}{D}\frac{dD}{dt} = \frac{1}{R_U}\frac{dR_U}{dt} - \frac{D}{R_U}\frac{d(R_R/D)}{dt} - \frac{D}{R_U}\frac{d(R_F/D)}{dt}$$

$$-\frac{D}{R_U}\frac{d(C_V/D)}{dt}. \qquad (3.16\text{A})$$

In this study attention has been focused upon the $d(R_F)/dt$ term, leaving the others for closer attention on some other occasion. In consideration of the formidable data problems and analytical problems involved it seemed advisable to consider the banks' demand function for vault cash as a problem worthy of separate investigation, in the same manner that study of changes in the reserve-requirement ratio was temporarily set aside.[6]

Determinants of the Free-Reserve Ratio

The actual free-reserve ratio at a given moment is determined by two main influences. One is the banks' demand for free reserves and the other is the rate at which Federal Reserve open-market operations add or withdraw unborrowed reserves. This view includes elements of both major explanations of bank behavior discussed in chapter ii. Open-market operations, which in reserve position doctrine are assumed to determine the

[3] Above, p. 34.

[4] Including the portion of vault cash that may be counted as part of legal reserves.

[5] Equation (3.9) on p. 35 above.

[6] Milton Friedman has since commented upon the implications of including vault cash in member-bank reserves. See his "Vault Cash and Free Reserves," *Journal of Political Economy*, LXIX, No. 2 (April, 1961), 181–82.

level of borrowing or free reserves, are introduced through the rate of change of unborrowed reserves. The possibility that reserve positions are influenced by other factors, as argued by critics of reserve position doctrine, is introduced through the concept of a desired reserve position that the banks attempt to maintain. The influence of the banks on the actual reserve position will be discussed first and the influence of open-market operations will be introduced later.

The principal hypothesis of this study is that the free-reserve ratio desired by banks is a function of market interest rates and the Federal Reserve discount rate.

$$\left(\frac{R_F}{D}\right)' = f(r_m, r_d, u). \tag{4.7}$$

In this expression u represents a collection of other variables that influence the demand for free reserves. The variables included in u are assumed to vary only slightly and randomly, although it is believed that empirical tests for the influence of some of them could be devised.

There are several ways of looking at the interest rates. The market interest rate, r_m, could be considered to represent the net yield of bank earning assets in general, or the marginal return on earning assets. In this view it would be a measure of the cost of holding excess reserves and of the gain to be expected from borrowing additional reserves in order to purchase more earning assets. In another view, r_m could be considered to be the yield of whatever instrument is the closest substitute for excess reserves, the Treasury bill for instance, that can be used for short-run adjustments to clearings and deposit changes. Various market interest rates are experimented with in the empirical part of the study to see which yield the best predictions. Furthermore, the form of the relationship in equation (4.7) has not been specified. One issue to be determined empirically is whether the ratio of market interest rates to the discount rate or the algebraic difference between them is relevant. Another is whether or not the absolute levels of market interest rates and the discount rate are significant. These questions are left open in the following discussion.

It might be objected that Regulation A, issued by the Board of Governors for the guidance of the Federal Reserve Banks in administering the discount function, interposes a non-price barrier that would make the volume of member-bank borrowing insensitive to changes in market interest rates and discount rates.[7] For example, E. C. Simmons has said, "It is

---

[7] Regulation A as revised in 1955 prescribes that member banks are to borrow only for short periods for the purpose of making reserve adjustments. Continuous borrowing is to be avoided, as is borrowing for profit. For recent Federal Reserve doctrine on control of member-bank borrowing, see Board of Governors of the Federal Reserve Sys-

quite clear that in reactivating the discount mechanism a deliberate choice was made to rely heavily on non-price rationing to control the amount of lending done by the central bank."[8] However, Regulation A prescribes a continuing operating policy, one that is not intended to vary in application over time. Furthermore, there is empirical evidence, to be discussed later, that the volume of borrowing since the revision of Regulation A in 1955 has in fact been sensitive to changes in rates.[9] The nominal discount rate need not be regarded as the full cost of borrowing in any case. The marginal disutility of overcoming the traditional reluctance to borrow and of risking disapproval at the discount window can be considered part of the actual discount rate that influences banks.

Work being done by George R. Morrison suggests that bank demand for free reserves should be considered as part of the general problem of bank portfolio management. Some of the variables with which he is concerned, and which are in effect impounded in u above, are the expected alternative net yields of various bank assets, the relative amounts of these assets in bank portfolios, and the relative riskiness of various assets.[10] These may well influence the banks' demand for free reserves but, in view of the possibility of benefiting from Morrison's study, no attempt was made in this study to measure their influence.

Changes in institutional arrangements that might change the demand

---

tem, *Forty-fourth Annual Report, Covering Operations for the Year 1957* (Washington: Board of Governors, 1958), pp. 7–18; "Discount Rate and the Discount Policy," *Business Review*, Federal Reserve Bank of Philadelphia, January, 1959, pp. 16–26; "Borrowing from the Fed," *Monthly Review*, Federal Reserve Bank of New York, September, 1959, pp. 138–42. See also Charls E. Walker, *Journal of Finance*, XII (May, 1957), 223–37; Charles R. Whittlesey, "Credit Policy at the Discount Window," *Quarterly Journal of Economics*, LXXIII (May, 1959), 207–16, 337–38; Robert V. Roosa, *Quarterly Journal of Economics*, LXXIII (May, 1959), 333–37; and George W. McKinney, Jr., *The Federal Reserve Discount Window* (New Brunswick, N.J.: Rutgers University Press, 1960). Regulation of the discount window is of course not new. For early discussions see, Board of Governors, *Twelfth Annual Report for 1925*, pp. 15–16; *Thirteenth Annual Report for 1926*, p. 3; *Fifteenth Annual Report for 1928*, pp. 7–8; Winfield W. Riefler, *Money Rates and Money Markets*, pp. 28–33; and W. Randolph Burgess, *The Reserve Banks and the Money Market*, pp. 59–65.

[8] Edward C. Simmons, "A Note on the Revival of Federal Reserve Discount Policy," *Journal of Finance*, XI (December, 1956), 414.

[9] Simmons also suggests that the traditional reluctance of banks to borrow may not be constant, which would reduce the stability of the relationship between demand for borrowed reserves and interest rates. He says, "In terms of a not inappropriate analogy the brakes may sometimes 'slip' and sometimes 'grab' " (*ibid.*, p. 418).

[10] George R. Morrison, "Portfolio Behavior of Banks" (Ph.D. dissertation, University of Chicago. In process, 1962).

for free reserves, such as the development of the Federal funds market and reduction of time required for check collection, are also impounded in u.

The desired free-reserve ratio for the system, like the reserve requirement-ratio, may be influenced by shifts in the distribution of deposits and reserves among the banks. According to the Federal Reserve Bank of New York: "Money market banks are generally more aggressive in seeking outlets for excess funds than are country banks, so that the significance of any national total of free reserves, or of net borrowed reserves, must depend in part upon the distribution of the total."[11] If the different classes of banks typically seek to maintain different ratios of free reserves to deposits, an increase in the share of total deposits held by the country banks, for instance, may increase the aggregate desired free-reserve ratio.[12] No allowance for this problem has been made in this study. However, empirical tests for the existence of a systematic relationship between the distribution of deposits and the free-reserve ratio could and should be made.[13]

The first assumption of this analysis is that each bank attempts to maintain some desired free-reserve position to provide for expected and unexpected clearings drains. This is similar to one of the basic assumptions of Meltzer's study of the French money supply.[14] Expected movements of deposits are also a variable in Morrison's study.[15] According to Morrison's hypothesis, experience of the banks with deposit changes, or clearings drains, may cause them to change the quantity of excess reserves they want to hold from time to time. In equation (4.7) above, expectations regarding clearings drains are treated as a constant. In an alternative form of the hypothesis, however, banks' expectations of clearings drains are assumed to have a regular seasonal pattern. In some months, accordingly, banks seek to maintain a larger free-reserve ratio

[11] "The Significance and Limitations of Free Reserves," *Monthly Review*, Federal Reserve Bank of New York, November, 1958, p. 163.

[12] It is interesting that Currie, dealing with the period before 1935, probably would have predicted the opposite effect. He asserted that country bankers were less averse to indebtedness than city bankers and that "country bankers, as a rule, have not stressed liquidity so much as city bankers" (Currie, *Supply and Control of Money*, p. 94).

[13] William R. Bryan has demonstrated that differences in characteristic responses of individual banks to changes in deposits and reserves make the distribution of deposits a significant influence on behavior of the system. See his "Bank Purchases of Earning Assets: A Decision Unit Model" (unpublished Ph.D. dissertation, University of Wisconsin, 1961).

[14] Meltzer, *Journal of Political Economy*, LXVII (June, 1959), 278. See above, p. 27.

[15] Morrison, "Portfolio Behavior of Banks."

with any given set of interest rates than in certain other months of the year. This alternative hypothesis is:

$$\left(\frac{R_F}{D}\right)' = f(r_m, r_d, S, u).$$ (4.8)

S represents the seasonal variation in expectations that modifies the free-reserve demand relationship.

THE RESERVE-ADJUSTMENT PROCESS

The objective of this section is to illustrate the process by which banks adjust reserve positions in response to changes in interest rates and in the rate at which the Federal Reserve provides unborrowed reserves. The three diagrams have been adapted from the stock-flow analysis employed by Milton Friedman in discussing capital theory.[16]

Three unobservable functional relationships illustrated in Figures 5, 6, and 7 are:

$$\left(\frac{R_F}{D}\right)' = f(r_m, r_d),$$ (4.9)

$$\left[\frac{d(R_F/D)}{dt}\right]' = g\left[\left(\frac{R_F}{D}\right)' - \left(\frac{R_F}{D}\right)\right],$$ (4.10)

and

$$\left[\frac{d(R_F/D)}{dt}\right]' = h\left(\frac{R_F}{D}, r_m, r_d\right).$$ (4.11)

Equation (4.9) expresses the banks' desired free-reserve ratio as a function of market interest rates and the discount rate. In equation (4.10) the desired rate of change of the free-reserve ratio is expressed as a function of the difference between the desired free-reserve ratio and the actual ratio. Equation (4.11) is derived from the other two by substituting (4.9) for $(R_F/D)'$ in (4.10).

In all three diagrams the reserve-requirement ratio and the discount rate are assumed to be constant. With market interest rates measured along the vertical axis of each diagram and with a fixed discount rate, the diagrams can be used to illustrate the effects of changes in market interest rates in relation to the discount rate under several hypotheses in addition to (4.9), such as,

$$\left(\frac{R_F}{D}\right)' = f(r_m - r_d),$$ (4.12)

or

$$\left(\frac{R_F}{D}\right)' = f\left(\frac{r_m}{r_d}\right).$$ (4.13)

[16] Milton Friedman, "Notes on Lectures in Price Theory" (mimeographed notes on lectures given January–June, 1951, in Economics 300*A* and 300*B*, at the University of Chicago), Part 2, pp. 112–14.

The total stock of unborrowed reserves is held constant in the first two diagrams. In the third diagram, the assumption of constant unborrowed reserves is relaxed in order to illustrate one more functional relationship:

$$\left[\frac{d\,(R_F/\,D)}{dt}\right]'' = k\left(\frac{R_F}{D},\ r_m,\ r_d,\ \frac{1}{R_U}\frac{dR_U}{dt}\right). \qquad (4.14)$$

According to equation (4.14), the banks' desired rate of change of the free-reserve ratio is a function of the level of the actual free-reserve ratio, market interest rates, the discount rate, and the rate at which the Federal Reserve injects or withdraws unborrowed reserves.

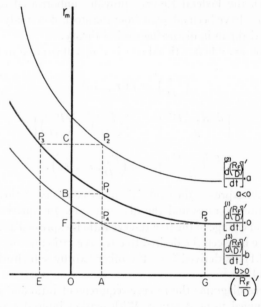

Fig. 5.—Long-run schedule of desired free-reserve ratios of all member banks as market interest rates vary. The discount rate, the average reserve-requirement ratio, and the stock of unborrowed reserves are assumed to be constant.

Curve (1) of Figure 5 is the banks' demand curve for free reserves, expressed as a ratio to total deposits. This is a demand schedule for a stock of reserves rather than for a flow of reserves per unit of time. For an illustration of its properties assume that initially the market interest rate is OB. The banks are satisfied with a ratio of free reserves to deposits of OA. If a change in the public's demand for money, for example, then causes market yields to rise to OC, the banks no longer want to maintain a free-reserve ratio of OA and would prefer a free-reserve ratio of OE. The banks can reach the new desired reserve position by reducing excess reserves, increasing borrowing, and buying earning assets (thus increasing deposits) until there no longer is any incentive to change. The process requires time because the adjustment efforts of some banks affect reserve positions of other banks, inducing those banks in turn to make changes in portfolios until everyone is satisfied. As the process goes on the number of banks that still have adjustments to make diminishes and the rate at which the banking system buys assets gradually falls to zero. If market interest rates fall to a lower level from the initial position the adjustments are made in the other direction; excess reserves increase, borrowing decreases, and deposits decline as the banks sell assets in order to change the free-reserve ratio.

The downward slope of the curve from left to right can be explained in terms of the costs of borrowing from the Federal Reserve and of holding excess reserves. As market yields rise in relation to the discount rate, borrowing becomes more profitable to the banks and the opportunity costs of holding excess reserves increase. Both of these effects of increases in market interest rates tend to cause banks to want to reduce the ratio of free reserves to deposits. At all points above the long-run demand curve the banks attempt to reduce the free-reserve ratio and at all points below it the banks attempt to increase the free-reserve ratio.

The curve can also be expected to be convex to the origin because it becomes progressively more difficult for the banks to reduce the free-reserve ratio as market interest rates rise. It becomes more and more difficult for the banks to operate without incurring penalties for reserve deficiencies as excess reserves are reduced. As borrowing increases, more and more banks approach the limits of borrowing set by administration of the discount window under Federal Reserve Regulation A.[17]

The desired rates at which the banks approach a new equilibrium point are represented by curves (2) and (3), each of which corresponds to a particular desired rate of change of the free-reserve ratio. Two examples are presented in the figure; in the first the banks are adjusting to an upward shift in the market interest rate and in the second they are adjusting to a decline in the market interest rate.

For the first example, the banks are initially in equilibrium at P_1. With an interest rate of OB they are satisfied to maintain a free-reserve ratio of OA. If there is an upward shift of the interest rate to OC the banks may be temporarily at P_2, on curve (2), where they attempt to reduce the free-

---

[17] An analysis of member-bank borrowing by Murray E. Polakoff, in which he employs indifference curves, profitability of borrowing, and a concept of "reluctance elasticity," would reinforce the arguments above about the curvature of the demand curve for free reserves (Polakoff, *Journal of Finance*, XV (March, 1960), 1–18).

reserve ratio at some rate a per unit of time. The greater the distance between P_2 and the new equilibrium point P_3, the more rapidly will the banks try to reduce the free reserve ratio. According to equation (4.10),

$$\left[\frac{d\,(R_F/D)}{dt}\right]' = g\left[\left(\frac{R_F}{D}\right)' - \left(\frac{R_F}{D}\right)\right]. \qquad (4.10)$$

In the specific case illustrated here the difference between the desired free-reserve ratio and the actual ratio is $OE - OA$ on the horizontal scale of Figure 5.

In the second example, the interest rate falls from OB to OF, and the banks temporarily hold the initial free-reserve ratio, OA, as represented by P_4 on curve (3). At this position the banks try to increase the free-reserve ratio at a rate of b per unit of time. The greater the difference between OG and OA the greater will be the rate at which the banks attempt to increase the free-reserve ratio by reducing borrowing and/or increasing excess reserves.

Short-run schedules of the desired rates of change of the free-reserve ratio for various combinations of interest rates and free-reserve ratios can be derived from the stock demand curve of Figure 5. On the flow-schedule diagram of Figure 6 each of the curves corresponds to a particular free-reserve ratio. For any combination of a market interest rate and a free-reserve ratio the rate at which the banks attempt to change the free-reserve ratio can be read from the horizontal axis. Any point at which a free-reserve curve crosses the vertical axis is a point on the long-run demand curve of Figure 5, for it identifies the rate of interest at which banks are satisfied to hold the given free-reserve ratio; the desired rate of change of the free-reserve ratio is zero. As interest rates increase on the vertical scale the curves intersecting the axis represent smaller and smaller free-reserve ratios. The particular three curves plotted in Figure 6 are for the free-reserve ratios used as examples in Figure 5. Thus curve (3) is for a free-reserve ratio of $(OA)_1$ as measured on the horizontal scale of Figure 5; curve (4) represents a free-reserve ratio of $(OE)_1$ on the horizontal scale of Figure 5; and curve (5) represents a free-reserve ratio of $(OG)_1$ on Figure 5. The parentheses and subscript 1 will be used to signify measurements on the horizontal scale of the first diagram. The interest rate scales on the vertical axes are the same for all three diagrams.

To retrace the first example worked out on Figure 5, the initial equilibrium position P_1 is on the vertical axis of Figure 6, signifying that at a market interest rate of OB the banks wish to maintain a free-reserve ratio of $(OA)_1$ (curve 3). If the interest rate rises to OC and the free-reserve ratio remains equal to $(OA)_1$ temporarily, the banks want to reduce the ratio.

The rate at which they desire to reduce it can be read from the horizontal scale as OH per unit of time. The new equilibrium position would be P_3 where the $R_F/D = (OE)_1$, curve intersects the vertical axis.

In the second example, in which r_m falls to OF while the free-reserve ratio remains temporarily at $(OA)_1$ (curve 3) the banks wish to increase the ratio at a rate of OI per unit of time. The new equilibrium position is at P_5, with a free reserve ratio of $(OG)_1$.

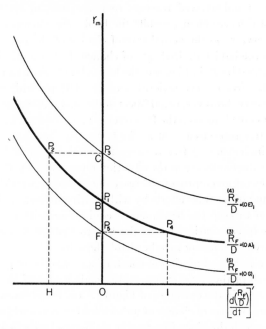

Fig. 6.—Schedules of desired rates of change of the free-reserve ratio for given actual free-reserve ratios as interest rates vary. The discount rate, the average reserve-requirement ratio, and the stock of unborrowed reserves are assumed to be constant.

Influence of Changes in Unborrowed Reserves

According to the argument thus far, a combination of r_m and R_F/D not on the long-run stock demand curve of Figure 5 would be expected to be merely a momentary situation on the path of adjustment from one equilibrium position to another. In the example presented in Figure 5, the banks for a brief time after an upward shift in the interest rate might be reducing the free-reserve ratio at a rate of a per unit of time, or OH in Figure 6, in order to approach the new equilibrium position, P_3. As they do this, required reserves and deposits rise. At some later time the actual free-reserve ratio will be closer to the desired one and the banks will be reducing the ratio at a slower rate. Eventually, the new equilibrium free-reserve ratio will be reached and the banks will no longer attempt to reduce the ratio. At the new position the volume of free reserves will be smaller than at the initial position, P_1, and total deposits will be larger than under the original conditions.

The adjustment process will proceed as described above only if the total stock of unborrowed reserves remains constant. If the stock of unborrowed reserves changes while the banks are attempting to change the free-reserve ratio the actual rate of change of the ratio may be different from the banks' desired rate of change. For example, in the situation represented by P_2 in Figure 6, the banks buy assets at a rate intended to reduce the free-reserve ratio at a rate of OH per unit of time. The Federal Reserve, however, could inject additional unborrowed reserves at a rate great enough to keep the free-reserve ratio constant by replenishing the banks' free reserves as fast as the banks use them and by providing additional increments of free reserves to match the growth in deposits. Similarly, if the banks are in the situation represented by P_4 in Figure 6, in which they are attempting to increase the free-reserve ratio, the Federal Reserve could offset their efforts by withdrawing unborrowed reserves. It is this power to keep the banks out of equilibrium with respect to their desired free-reserve ratios that is the key to Federal Reserve influence over the rate of change of member-bank deposits.

In Figure 7 the assumption of constant unborrowed reserves has been relaxed. Each of the three curves corresponds to one of the free-reserve ratios employed in the examples of Figures 5 and 6 and contains all of the combinations of rates of change of unborrowed reserves and market interest rates at which the given free-reserve ratio would remain constant. The initial equilibrium position employed in the preceding illustrations is again P_1, with a market interest rate of OB and a free-reserve ratio of $(OA)_1$ (as measured on the horizontal scale of Figure 5), represented by curve (7). The banks are satisfied to maintain the free reserve ratio of $(OA)_1$ and so the rate of change of unborrowed reserves is equal to zero. From equation (3.16) it can be seen that in this situation the rate of change of deposits is also zero. For,

$$\frac{1}{D}\frac{dD}{dt} = \frac{1}{R_U}\frac{dR_U}{dt} - \frac{D}{R_U}\frac{d(R_R/D)}{dt} - \frac{D}{R_U}\frac{d(R_F/D)}{dt}. \quad (3.16)$$

Because the reserve-requirement ratio has been assumed to be constant in all of these illustrations, the reserve-requirement ratio term can be omitted.

For a different free-reserve ratio, say $(OG)_1$, (curve 6), to be maintained at the same interest rate, OB, unborrowed reserves would have to be increasing at a rate of OL per unit of time, measured on the horizontal scale of Figure 7, in order to offset the banks' efforts to reduce the ratio. In the situation represented by P_6, deposits would also be increasing at a rate of OL. If, on the other hand, a free-reserve ratio of $(OE)_1$, (curve 8), were to be maintained with an interest rate of OB, unborrowed reserves and deposits would have to be contracting at a rate of OK on the horizontal scale

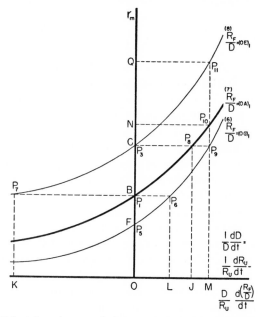

Fig. 7.—Schedules of rates of change of deposits and unborrowed reserves with selected free ratios as market interest rates vary. The discount rate and the average reserve-requirement ratio are assumed to be constant.

of Figure 7, in order to offset the banks' efforts to increase the ratio. Points P_6 and P_7 are positions of secondary equilibrium; combinations of interest rates and rates of change of unborrowed reserves at which particular free-reserve ratios will remain constant. At any given interest rate, the higher the rate of change of unborrowed reserves the larger will be the free-reserve ratio maintained by the banks.

Denoting the desired free-reserve ratio at a point of secondary equilibrium by $(R_F/D)''$,

$$\left(\frac{R_F}{D}\right)'' = j\left(r_m, r_d, \frac{1}{R_U}\frac{dR_U}{dt}\right). \tag{4.15}$$

The banks' desired rate of change of the free-reserve ratio would then be related to the difference between the actual free-reserve ratio and the equilibrium ratio for the prevailing interest rates and the current rate of change of unborrowed reserves.

$$\left[\frac{d(R_F/D)}{dt}\right]'' = 1\left[\left(\frac{R_F}{D}\right)'' - \left(\frac{R_F}{D}\right)\right]. \tag{4.16}$$

Substituting equation (4.15) for $(R_F/D)''$ in (4.16) completes the derivation of equation (4.14),

$$\left[\frac{d(R_F/D)}{dt}\right]'' = k\left(\frac{R_F}{D}, r_m, r_d, \frac{1}{R_U}\frac{dR_U}{dt}\right). \tag{4.14}$$

Using Figure 7 to illustrate the effects of a change of interest rates, assume again the initial equilibrium situation, P_1. The interest rate then shifts upward to OC, as in the first example worked out on Figures 5 and 6. The new long-run equilibrium situation would be P_3, with a free-reserve ratio of $(OE)_1$, (curve 8), as can be seen from Figures 5 and 6. If unborrowed reserves remained constant the banks would in time acquire enough assets to reduce the free-reserve ratio to $(OE)_1$, after which there would be no incentive to change until interest rates changed again. Deposits would grow in the time the shift of free-reserve ratios was occurring. This is the adjustment process illustrated in Figures 5 and 6. The Federal Reserve could, however, cause the free-reserve ratio to remain at $(OA)_1$, despite the shift of interest rate, by increasing the rate of change of unborrowed reserves to OJ per unit of time. If the Federal Reserve were to increase the rate of change of unborrowed reserves even more, for example to OM, the free-reserve ratio would actually increase after the upward shift of interest rates, despite the banks' efforts to reduce it.

At every one of the secondary equilibrium positions the rate of change of unborrowed reserves and the rate of change of deposits are equal, because the free-reserve ratio is constant. If the rate of change of unborrowed reserves at a given moment and with given interest rates is something less than the rate required to maintain the actual free-reserve ratio, the rate of change of the free-reserve ratio at that moment will be negative. The rate of change of deposits consequently will be greater than the rate of change of unborrowed reserves. This proposition can be illustrated by assuming the banks to be initially at P_9 with an interest rate of OC, a free-reserve ratio of $(OG)_1$, (curve 6), and with unborrowed reserves and deposits both growing at a rate of OM. If the rate of growth of unborrowed reserves should suddenly drop to OJ, the free-reserve ratio might remain momentarily unchanged. At that moment, however, the rate of change of the free-reserve ratio would become negative, as the banks started to shift toward the free-reserve ratio $(OA)_1$, (curve 7). The rate of change of deposits would be greater than the rate of change of unborrowed reserves and would be somewhere between OJ and OM. As time passed the free-reserve ratio would contract at a smaller and smaller rate, and the rate of growth of deposits would gradually diminish until it approached equality with the rate of growth of unborrowed reserves again at OJ.

SOME IMPLICATIONS FOR OPEN-MARKET OPERATIONS

A theory of deposit expansion should supply an answer to the question: At what rate will total deposits grow if Federal Reserve open-market operations increase unborrowed reserves of the member banks at some given rate? The apparatus presented in Figure 7 can be used to demonstrate some of the difficulties of answering that question.

Assume that the market interest rate is OC; that unborrowed reserves are increasing at a rate of OJ per unit of time, say 3 per cent per year; and that the actual free-reserve ratio is the one represented by (curve 7), $(OA)_1$. Under these conditions deposits are also growing at a rate of OJ, or 3 per cent per year. At the same interest rate, if unborrowed reserves were increasing at OM per unit of time, say 5 per cent per year, and the free-reserve ratio was the one represented by curve (6), $(OG)_1$, deposits would be growing at 5 per cent per year. If the central bank wanted to increase the rate of deposit growth from the initial 3 per cent annual rate to a 5 per cent annual rate, however, it could not immediately achieve its goal by increasing the rate of growth of unborrowed reserves to 5 per cent per year. One of the immediate effects of an increase in the rate of change of unborrowed reserves under the assumed conditions would be an increase in the rate of change of the free-reserve ratio, $d(R_F/D)/dt$, from zero to some positive rate. Therefore, according to equation (3.16), the rate of change of deposits must be less than the rate of change of unborrowed reserves for a time. During the time required for the free-reserve ratio to increase to $(OG)_1$, (curve 6), the rate of deposit change would be somewhere between 3 and 5 per cent per year, and would approach 5 per cent as the free-reserve ratio approached $(OG)_1$. In order to accomplish the desired change in rate of deposit growth more promptly, the central bank would have to increase the banks' stock of unborrowed reserves for a time at some rate greater than OM, perhaps at a 7 per cent annual rate for example and then gradually reduce the rate of change of unborrowed reserves to OM, or 5 per cent per year, as the free-reserve ratio approached $(OG)_1$, (curve 6).

The preceding example illustrates the problem of changing the rate of deposit growth with other conditions remaining unchanged. There also is a problem in maintaining a constant rate of deposit growth in the face of changes in other conditions influencing bank behavior. For example, assume that with an interest rate of OC deposits are growing at the rate desired by the central bank, OM, or 5 per cent per year, as unborrowed reserves increase at a 5 per cent annual rate. Then assume that the market interest rate shifts up to OQ, providing incentive for the banks to reduce the free-reserve ratio. As the banks increase their borrowing and/or reduce their excess reserves in order to reduce the free-reserve ratio, they supplement for a time the unborrowed reserves provided by the central bank. Therefore, if the central bank continues to increase unborrowed reserves at the original 5 per cent annual rate, OM, deposits for a time will grow at a somewhat greater rate. As the free-reserve ratio approaches the value represented by curve (8), $(OE)_1$, the rate of deposit growth will approach its original value, OM, again. In this case, the central bank would have had to reduce the rate of change of unborrowed reserves temporarily in order to prevent the shift in interest rate from inducing an increase in rate of deposit growth.

Behavior of the deposit expansion mechanism defined by the schedules of Figure 7 and by equation (3.16) appears to be consistent with the behavior of member-bank deposits and unborrowed reserves plotted in Figure 3 and discussed on pages 37–41 above.

CONTROL CHARACTERISTICS OF THE MECHANISM

The expected responses of the mechanism to open-market operations and to interest rate changes can be summarized as follows:

1. If open-market operations increase the rate at which unborrowed reserves are provided to the banks, and if market interest rates remain constant, the free-reserve ratio and the rate of change of deposits will rise. The rate of change of deposits will not rise as rapidly as the rate of change of unborrowed reserves because some of the additional reserves will be used by the banks to increase the free-reserve ratio (by reducing borrowings and increasing excess reserves). Eventually, assuming no further change in the rate at which open-market operations provide reserves, the free-reserve ratio will stop rising and the rate of change of deposits will be equal to the rate of change of unborrowed reserves, in percentage terms.

2. If open-market operations reduce the rate at which unborrowed reserves are provided to the banks, or contract the supply of reserves, the free-reserve ratio and the rate of change of deposits will decline. The change in rate of deposit expansion (or contraction) will lag behind the

change in rate of expansion (or contraction) of unborrowed reserves, as the banks increase their borrowing and reduce excess reserves.

3. If market interest rates shift to a higher level, with open-market operations supplying unborrowed reserves at a constant rate, the free-reserve ratio will decline. During the time the free-reserve ratio is declining, the rate of deposit change will rise for a while and then decline to its original rate, because the banks will be supplementing reserves supplied through open-market operations by increasing borrowings and reducing excess reserves.

4. If market interest rates fall to a lower level, with open-market operations supplying unborrowed reserves at a constant rate, the free-reserve ratio will rise and the rate of deposit change will be smaller than the rate of change of unborrowed reserves for a time, in percentage terms.

IMPLICATIONS FOR USE OF FREE-RESERVE LEVEL AS AN INDICATOR OF MONETARY POLICY

Two major arguments against use of the free-reserve level as an indicator of monetary policy can be drawn from Figure 7. The first of them is that a given rate of change of deposits can be consistent with various free-reserve ratios. For example, a rate of deposit change of OM is shown to occur with free-reserve ratios of $(OE)_1$, $(OA)_1$, $(OG)_1$, and many more that are not plotted. The ones plotted range from negative to positive values.

Although the first argument might be accepted it still might be argued that a change in free-reserve level or free-reserve ratio would be a significant indication of a change in monetary policy. Such an argument implies that the Federal Reserve deliberately sets the free-reserve level. Hobart C. Carr, for example, discusses a technique for deducing whether a given observed change in free-reserve level was intended by the Federal Reserve or whether an error might have been made in attempting to offset some of the market factors affecting reserves.[18] Putting aside the question of whether or not open market operations can offset the market factors well enough to produce a desired effect upon the rate of change of unborrowed reserves, a change in the free-reserve ratio in the deposit expansion mechanism of Figure 7 still would not be a dependable indication of a change in the degree of restrictiveness of central-bank policy. The crucial question is whether a given change in free-reserve ratio occurs at the initiative of the Federal Reserve or at the initiative of the banks.

A change in free-reserve ratio initiated by the Federal Reserve was il-

---

[18] Carr, *Journal of Finance*, XIV (December, 1959), 504–19.

lustrated above when it was assumed that the Federal Reserve increased the rate of growth of unborrowed reserves in order to increase the rate of growth of deposits, with interest rates remaining unchanged. One of the results of the action was an increase in the free-reserve ratio. In this case the rise in free-reserve ratio could be properly interpreted as an indication of an easing in the degree of restrictiveness of monetary policy. A less ambiguous indication, of course, was provided by the change in rate of growth of deposits.

A change in free-reserve ratio initiated by the banks was illustrated above by an upward shift of market interest rates with the Federal Reserve holding the rate of change of unborrowed reserves constant. The banks were induced to reduce the free-reserve ratio, a change that should have been interpreted as a tightening in policy, to be consistent with the preceding case. Nevertheless, a result of the shift in free-reserve ratio was an increase in the rate of deposit growth for a time, so that monetary policy was in effect eased. If the rate of change of unborrowed reserves and interest rates change at the same time, as might be expected at a cyclical turning point, a change of free-reserve ratio becomes even more difficult to interpret.[19]

DETERMINATION OF MARKET INTEREST RATES

To this point in the discussion, it has been assumed that market interest rates are autonomously determined, and so changes in the free-reserve ratios of the banks have been viewed merely as adjustments to changes in market interest rates relative to the discount rate. Now it is necessary to examine the implications of this assumption more carefully.

An alternative hypothesis, and one that was central to several of the reserve position studies reviewed in chapter ii, is that the level of member-bank free reserves is one of the principal influences determining market rates of interest, especially short-term rates.[20] According to the alternative hypothesis, an observed correlation between the free-reserve ratio and market interest rates would be attributed to the influence of the free-reserve ratio on interest rates. The argument of this study, to the contrary, is that market interest rates are not determined by the level of the

[19] The argument has been made here in terms of free-reserve ratios rather than free-reserve levels and in rates of growth of member-bank deposits rather than in rates of growth of the total money supply. Making allowances for the differences in concept, however, would not have contradicted the argument.

[20] Although some of the studies referred to use the volume of member-bank borrowing rather than the level of free reserves, the arguments are the same.

free-reserve ratio but are instead the resultant of the whole complex of supply-and-demand schedules in the markets for money and loanable funds. *Changes* in the free-reserve ratio, however, do influence market interest rates as the banks buy or sell assets in order to adjust their reserve positions.

To illustrate the distinction between the level of the free-reserve ratio and a change in the ratio, in regard to influence upon market interest rates, assume that the member banks suddenly have an increase in free reserves as the result of a lowering of reserve requirements. If the banks choose merely to hold the additional reserves without using them there is no reason for interest rates to change, for market supplies of assets have not been changed. According to the argument of Figures 5 and 6, however, if the banks had been maintaining the equilibrium free-reserve ratio for the prevailing interest rate before the change in reserve requirements, the actual reserve ratio immediately after the change will be greater than the desired ratio. In attempting to reduce the free-reserve ratio the banks then buy assets, tending to depress interest rates, perhaps with particular influence upon rates for the types of securities used by the banks for adjustment purposes. If interest rates decline, the desired free-reserve ratio of the banks will increase, according to curve (1) of Figure 5. Thus the new equilibrium reserve ratio after the banks have completed the process of adjustment will have some value between the initial ratio and the one reached immediately after the reserve-requirement change.

It might be argued that other participants in the market realize that free reserves of the banks have been increased by the reserve-requirement reduction and consequently change their demand-and-supply schedules enough to reduce interest rates before the banks have begun to use the newly acquired reserves. However, such an effect would be based upon expectations that the banks would in time use the reserves to buy assets and hence is not really an exception to the argument presented above.

The case in which interest rates and the free-reserve ratio are influenced by open-market operations of the central bank is somewhat more complicated but can be illustrated on Figure 7, retracing the case on pages 57 and 58 above of an increase in the rate of growth of unborrowed reserves. The system is initially in equilibrium with a market interest rate of OC; with unborrowed reserves and deposits both growing at a rate of OJ per unit of time, or 3 per cent per year; and with an actual free-reserve ratio of $(OA)_1$, represented by curve (7). If the central bank then increases the rate of growth of unborrowed reserves to OM, or 5 per cent per year, and if the interest rate remains constant, the rate of growth of deposits will increase to 5 per cent per year and the free-reserve ratio will increase to

$(OG)_1$, represented by curve (6), after a period of adjustment. The assumption of a constant market interest rate in this case actually is an assumption that demand-and-supply schedules of other participants will change exactly enough to offset the influence upon interest rates of the increase in rate of purchases of assets by the central bank and the member banks. If it is assumed instead that the demand-and-supply schedules of the others remain constant the following effects would be expected: The increase in the rate of open-market purchases of the central bank, the increase in the rate of asset purchases by the banks, and the increase in rate of growth of deposits would depress interest rates. The desired free-reserve ratio of the banks would increase as the market interest rate declined. The eventual new position of secondary equilibrium, therefore, would not be P_9 with a free-reserve ratio of $(OG)_1$, but would be on some lower curve, representing a larger free-reserve ratio (not plotted). After the increase in rate of growth of unborrowed reserves and deposits the free-reserve ratio is larger than it had been before and the interest rate is lower, but the changes in both of these are results of the initial change in rate of growth of unborrowed reserves at the volition of the central bank.

Introducing the influence of central-bank action upon market interest rates, as was done above, reinforces the tendency of the banking system to offset automatically to some degree a change in monetary policy expressed through open-market operations, if the hypothesis of this study is correct. With constant interest rates, there is a time lag between an increase in the rate of growth of unborrowed reserves and the resulting change in rate of growth of deposits, because some of the additional reserves provided through open-market operations are used to increase the free-reserve ratio. If market interest rates decline when the rates of growth of unborrowed reserves and deposits increase, the induced change in free-reserve ratio, as we have just seen, is greater than if interest rates had remained constant, hence using up or releasing more reserves and probably increasing the time lag.

TREATMENT OF EXCESS RESERVES AND BORROWINGS SEPARATELY OR AS COMBINED IN FREE RESERVES

To combine the excess-reserve ratio and the ratio of borrowings to deposits in the free-reserve ratio is appropriate in the accounting sense used in equations (3.15) and (3.16), but the combination in the behavioral equations is more open to question. The treatment in equations (4.3–4.15) and in the diagrams rests upon assumptions that the desired excess-reserve ratios and desired borrowings ratios are functionally related to the same variables and that the relationships are linear.

One way the demand functions for the excess-reserve ratios and borrowings ratios may be combined is:

$$\left(\frac{R_F}{D}\right)' = f(r_m, r_d), \tag{4.9}$$

$$\left(\frac{R_E}{D}\right)' = g(r_m, r_d), \tag{4.17}$$

$$\left(\frac{R_B}{D}\right)' = h(r_m, r_d), \tag{4.18}$$

$$\left(\frac{R_F}{D}\right)' = a + b\,r_m + c\,r_d, \tag{4.19}$$

$$\left(\frac{R_E}{D}\right)' = e + i\,r_m + j\,r_d, \tag{4.20}$$

$$\left(\frac{R_B}{D}\right)' = k + l\,r_m + n\,r_d, \tag{4.21}$$

and

$$\left(\frac{R_F}{D}\right)' = (e - k) + (i - l)\,r_m + (j - n)\,r_d. \tag{4.22}$$

V

Empirical Evidence

INTRODUCTION

THE KEY to the hypotheses developed in chapter iv was the desired free-reserve ratio of the member banks, $(R_F/D)'$. Since the desired free-reserve ratio cannot be observed directly, one of the principal problems of the empirical work was to infer behavior of the desired ratio from behavior of variables that can be observed, such as the actual free-reserve ratio, interest rates, and member-bank deposits.

In one group of experiments, attempts were made to estimate rates of change of member-bank deposits from actual free-reserve ratios, market interest rates, and the discount rate. For these tests it was hypothesized that the desired free-reserve ratio is a function of market interest rates and the discount rate, and that the rate at which banks attempt to change the free-reserve ratio is a function of the difference between the desired free-reserve ratio and their actual reserve position. The relationships used were:

$$\left(\frac{R_F}{D}\right)' = f(r_m, r_d), \qquad (4.9)$$

$$\left[\frac{d(R_F/D)}{dt}\right]' = g\left[\left(\frac{R_F}{D}\right)' - \left(\frac{R_F}{D}\right)\right], \qquad (4.10)$$

and

$$\left[\frac{d(R_F/D)}{dt}\right]' = h\left(\frac{R_F}{D}, r_m, r_d\right). \qquad (4.11)$$

Because the banks buy or sell assets in adjusting their free-reserve ratios and hence change the volume of deposits, it was assumed that a desired rate of change of deposits could be substituted for the desired rate of change of the free-reserve ratio in (4.11) to obtain:

$$\left(\frac{1}{D}\frac{dD}{dt}\right)' = i\left(\frac{R_F}{D}, r_m, r_d\right). \qquad (5.1)$$

In another version, the rate of change of unborrowed reserves adjusted for reserve-requirement changes was added:[1]

$$\left(\frac{1}{D}\frac{dD}{dt}\right)' = j\left[\frac{R_F}{D}, r_m, r_d, \left(\frac{1}{R_U}\frac{dR_U}{dt}\right)^*\right] \qquad (5.2)$$

[1] The asterisk in (5.2) and later equations is to signify that the rate of change of unborrowed reserves has been adjusted for changes in the reserve requirement ratio:

$$\left(\frac{1}{R_U}\frac{dR_U}{dt}\right)^* = \frac{1}{R_U}\frac{dR_U}{dt} - \frac{D}{R_U}\frac{d(R_R/D)}{dt}.$$

Assuming that the actual rates of change of deposits were equal to the desired rates, linear regression equations of the following form were fitted by the method of least squares:

$$\frac{1}{D}\frac{dD}{dt} = a + b\left(\frac{R_F}{D}\right) + c\,r_m + e\,r_d \qquad (5.3)$$

or

$$\frac{1}{D}\frac{dD}{dt} = a + b\left(\frac{R_F}{D}\right) + c\,r_m + e\,r_d + h\left(\frac{1}{R_U}\frac{dR_U}{dt}\right)^*. \qquad (5.4)$$

Linear equations were similarly derived for prediction of the rate of change of the free-reserve ratio and of the free-reserve ratio itself. Equations for predicting the rate of change of the free-reserve ratio were drawn from (4.11) above and from (4.14):

$$\left[\frac{d(R_F/D)}{dt}\right] = k\left[\frac{R_F}{D}, r_m, r_d, \left(\frac{1}{R_U}\frac{dR_U}{dt}\right)^*\right]. \qquad (4.14)$$

Equations for predicting the free-reserve ratios were drawn from (4.9), (4.8), and (4.15), assuming in each case that the desired ratios could be estimated from the observed ratios:

$$\left(\frac{R_F}{D}\right)' = f(r_m, r_d), \qquad (4.9)$$

$$\left(\frac{R_F}{D}\right)' = f(r_m, r_d, S), \qquad (4.8)$$

and

$$\left(\frac{R_F}{D}\right)'' = j\left[r_m, r_d, \left(\frac{1}{R_U}\frac{dR_U}{dt}\right)^*\right]. \qquad (4.15)$$

The deposit and reserves data used were monthly and semimonthly averages of daily figures obtained from the Board of Governors Release J. 1, entitled "Deposits, Reserves, and Borrowings of Member Banks." The deposit concept employed was net member-bank demand deposits subject to reserve requirements plus time deposits subject to reserve requirements. The monthly rates of change were calculated in the following manner.

1. The mean of the daily averages of the particular item, deposits for example, in the two semimonthly periods on either side of a given date was taken as an estimate of the value of the item at that date.

2. The difference between the estimate of deposits at the end of a given month and at the beginning of that month was assumed to be the rate of change of deposits at midmonth, dD/dt.

3. To obtain $(1/D)(dD/dt)$, the estimate of dD/dt obtained as above was then divided by the estimated value of D at midmonth.

The interest rates used were monthly averages of the new issue rate on 91-day Treasury bills, the market yield on 3–5-year Treasury securities, and the New York discount rate, all from the *Federal Reserve Bulletin*.

EXPERIMENTS IN PREDICTING THE RATE OF CHANGE OF DEPOSITS

Initially, this study was intended as an examination of the proposition that when free reserves are large the rate of growth of deposits tends to be high and that when free reserves are negative, or "net borrowed," the rate of change of deposits is small or negative.[2] The fact that a given level of free reserves may be associated with various rates of deposit change might be explained, according to the initial hypothesis, by differences in market interest rates and the discount rate. Thus, with a given free-reserve level, the rate of deposit change would be expected to be larger when market rates were high relative to the discount rate than when market rates were low. Several variations of equations (5.3) and (5.4) were tested by means of linear multiple regressions, employing various deposit series, interest rates, and time periods.[3] Figures 8 and 9 illustrate the results of some of these tests. Superficially at least, equation (T6) of Figure 9 would appear to confirm the hypothesis, with required reserves substituted for deposits. Looking behind the apparent relationships, however, raised questions about what determines the free-reserve ratio, which had been used as an independent variable in equation (T6) and the other tests of the series. When the rate of change of unborrowed reserves was included in the regression equations, as in (5.4), it appeared to account for most of the variation in rate of deposit change.[4] This suggested that the observed correlation of the rate of deposit change with the free-reserve ratio and interest rates might be the result of a relationship among the free-reserve ratio, interest rates, and the rate of change of unborrowed reserves. Attention was then directed to the determinants of the free-reserve ratio and its rate of change.

OBSERVATIONS WITH ANNUAL DATA, 1929–59

Annual averages of the ratio of free reserves to total deposits minus required reserves for the year 1929 through 1959 were plotted in a scatter diagram with the ratio of the Treasury-bill rate to the New York discount rate (Fig. 10). A free-hand curve drawn approximately through averages of groups of the original points resembles the long-run stock demand curve of Figure 5 in chapter iv. In Figure 11 the same points were plotted with

[2] See Federal Reserve Bank of New York, *Monthly Review*, November, 1958, p. 164.

[3] See Appendix A for additional details.

[4] Equations (T7), (T8), and (T9), Appendix A.

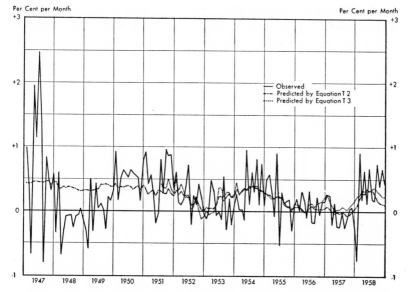

Fig. 8.—Observed and predicted monthly rates of change of seasonally adjusted member-bank demand deposits, 1947–58. The deposits used were monthly averages of daily demand deposits minus cash items in process of collection and treasury balances, in accordance with the Federal Reserve concept of "demand deposits adjusted." The free-reserve ratio was the ratio of free reserves to total reserves, R_F/R, in monthly averages of daily figures. The interest rates were the average new issue rate on 91-day Treasury bills, r_b, and the New York discount rate, r_d.

Equation (T2) was fitted for January, 1947, through December, 1958, and had a coefficient of multiple determination, R^2, of 0.10.

$$\frac{1}{D}\frac{dD}{dt} = 0.381 + 0.039\frac{R_F}{R} - 0.0710\,r_d - 0.0324\,r_b. \quad (T2)$$

Equation (T3) was fitted for July, 1951, through December, 1958, in order to avoid the influence of the bond-support program of the Federal Reserve before the Federal Reserve-Treasury accord. Its coefficient of multiple determination was 0.17.

$$\frac{1}{D}\frac{dD}{dt} = 0.00486 + 0.0796\frac{R_F}{R} + 0.223\frac{r_b}{r_d}. \quad (T3)$$

Sources: J.1 Releases of the Board of Governors of the Federal Reserve System and the *Federal Reserve Bulletin*. Deposit series seasonally adjusted by the Federal Reserve Bank of St. Louis.

Free Reserves and the Money Supply

the interest ratio on logarithmic scale. If the call-loan rate is substituted for the bill rate in 1929 and 1930, as has been done in the points marked with asterisks, the free-reserve ratio more nearly approaches the curve. These two scatter diagrams are much like those Jan Tinbergen, J. J.

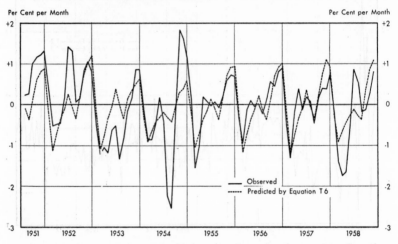

FIG. 9.—Observed and predicted monthly rates of change of member-bank required reserves, July, 1951–December, 1958. The rates of change were monthly percentage changes in monthly averages of daily required reserves and were smoothed with a three-term weighted moving average with weights of $\frac{1}{4}$, $\frac{1}{2}$, and $\frac{1}{4}$. The interest rates were the Treasury bill rate and the New York discount rate. The deposits in the free-reserve ratio were monthly averages of total member-bank deposits subject to reserve requirements. The required reserves were not seasonally adjusted, but seasonal weights were incorporated in the regression coefficients estimated for the interest ratios in regression equation (T6):

$$\frac{1}{R_R}\frac{dR_R}{dt} = -0.546 + 1.00\frac{R_F}{D} + 0.372\left(\frac{r_b}{r_d}\right)_1 - 0.649\left(\frac{r_b}{r_d}\right)_2$$

$$-0.189\left(\frac{r_b}{r_d}\right)_3 + 0.206\left(\frac{r_b}{r_d}\right)_4 + 0.450\left(\frac{r_b}{r_d}\right)_5 + 0.828\left(\frac{r_b}{r_d}\right)_6$$

$$+0.493\left(\frac{r_b}{r_d}\right)_7 + 0.193\left(\frac{r_b}{r_d}\right)_8 + 0.741\left(\frac{r_b}{r_d}\right)_9 + 1.27\left(\frac{r_b}{r_d}\right)_{10}$$

$$+1.48\left(\frac{r_b}{r_d}\right)_{11} + 1.45\left(\frac{r_b}{r_d}\right)_{12}.$$

Each interest ratio was assumed to be zero except in the month indicated by its subscript. The coefficient of multiple determination, R^2, was 0.49.

Sources: J.1 Releases of the Board of Governors of the Federal Reserve System and the *Federal Reserve Bulletin*.

Polak, and W. H. White plotted in deriving relationships between net indebtedness, or free reserves, and market interest rates.[5]

EXPERIMENTS WITH MONTHLY DATA, 1947–58

The variables used in the tests with monthly data were the Treasury bill rate, r_b, the rate on 3–5-year governments, r_{3-5}, the ratio of free reserves to total deposits subject to reserve requirements, R_F/D, and the

[5] Tinbergen, *Business Cycles in the United States*, p. 84; and Polak and White, *International Monetary Fund Staff Papers*, IV (August, 1955), 424.

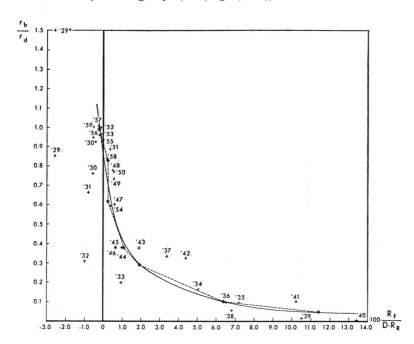

FIG. 10.—Annual average free-reserve ratios and ratios of bill rate to the New York discount rate, 1929–59. Required reserves were subtracted from deposits in the free-reserve ratios in order to adjust for changes in reserve requirements over the period covered. The encircled points are averages of the points falling within selected ranges of the interest ratios. In the points for 1929 and 1930 that are marked with asterisks the call-loan rate was substituted for the rate on short-term Treasury securities, on the assumption that in those years call loans were more generally used by the banks for adjusting reserve positions than were government securities.

Sources: J.1 Releases of the Board of Governors of the Federal Reserve System; *Banking and Monetary Statistics;* and the *Federal Reserve Bulletin.*

rate of change of unborrowed reserves adjusted for changes in the required reserves ratio, hereafter denoted by ϕ for convenience.

$$\phi = \frac{1}{R_U}\frac{dR_U}{dt} - \frac{D}{R_U}\frac{d(R_R/D)}{dt}. \tag{5.5}$$

Most of the basic data appear in Appendix D. The linear multiple regression equations of this series of tests appear in Appendixes B and C. The

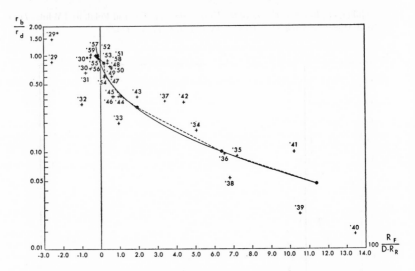

Fig. 11.—Annual average free-reserve ratios and ratios of bill rate to the New York discount rate, 1929–59 with interest ratios on logarithmic scale. This scatter diagram is like Figure 10 in every respect except that the interest ratios have been plotted on a logarithmic scale.

findings of this series of tests can be illustrated well by two of the regression equations and by Figure 12. The standard error of each coefficient appears directly under it in parentheses.

$$100\left(\frac{R_F}{D}\right) = \underset{(0.0200)}{0.835} + \underset{(0.0939)}{0.0985}\ r_d - \underset{(0.0711)}{0.464}\ r_b, \tag{T11}$$

and

$$100\left(\frac{R_F}{D}\right)_t = \underset{(0.0180)}{1.409} - \underset{(0.129)}{0.549}\left(\frac{r_b}{r_d}\right)_t$$
$$- \underset{(0.032)}{0.321}(r_{3-5})_t + \underset{(0.0185)}{0.0726}\left(\frac{\phi_{t-1}+\phi_t}{2}\right). \tag{T22}$$

Equation (T11), which was the simplest one tried, had a coefficient of multiple determination (R^2) of 0.62. The regression coefficient for the discount rate was not significant, but the bill rate and the discount rate were so highly correlated with each other that this could not be considered a conclusive test.[6] Equation (T22) had a coefficient of multiple determi-

[6] The coefficient of partial correlation for the discount rate was 0.089, as compared to a partial correlation of 0.48 for the bill rate. The coefficient of simple correlation between the bill rate and the discount rate was 0.93. The sign of the regression coefficient for the discount rate, however, was consistent with the hypothesis.

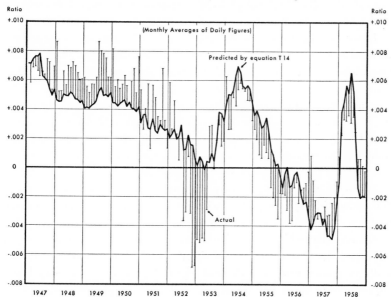

FIG. 12.—Actual free-reserve ratios and ratios predicted by equation (T14). Monthly averages of daily figures. Regression equation (T14) was one of several fitted to data for January, 1947, through December, 1958.

$$100 \left(\frac{R_F}{D}\right) = 0.839 + \underset{[0.0073]}{0.0955} \; r_d - \underset{[0.232]}{0.463} \; r_b$$
$$+ \underset{[0.0045]}{9.01} \; \frac{d(R_F/D)}{dt}. \tag{T14}$$

The coefficient of multiple determination, R^2, was 0.629. The part of the net variance explained by each variable (the coefficient of partial correlation squared) appears in the brackets. The coefficients of partial correlation for the discount rate and for the rate of change of the free-reserve ratio (the change in the monthly average for each month to that of the next month) were not significantly different from zero below the 30 per cent level. See Appendix C for additional details.

nation of 0.70, the highest for any test of this series. The standard errors of the coefficients indicate that all three of the independent variables in equation (T22) were significant.

The ratio of bill rate to discount rate and the rate on 3–5-year governments appear in the same equation in order to test a hypothesis that interest rates are involved in two ways. First, the spread between bill rate and discount rate, or their ratio, may influence the banks' choices between borrowing and selling bills when reserve adjustments become necessary. Second, the absolute level of market interest rates may influence the choice between holding excess reserves or holding earning assets.

Equation (T22) was one of several in which time lags were experimented with. All variables with a subscript t pertain to the same month. One with a subscript $t - 1$ pertains to the month preceding month t. The rate of change of unborrowed reserves, ϕ, in the month for which R_F/D was predicted had been found to have very little influence, but introducing it with a lag of one month, or using the average of ϕ for the current month and one month preceding, as was done in (T22), roughly tripled its influence. Nevertheless, the influence of the rate of change of unborrowed reserves was much less than was that of interest rates.

When the free-reserve ratios predicted by the regression equations of this series of tests were plotted with respect to time and were compared with the actual ratios, as in Figure 12, it appeared that structural shifts may have occurred in the relationships within the period included, or that the equations were faulty. The residuals of all of the equations were serially correlated much like those of Figure 12. Termination of the bond-support policy of the Federal Reserve in 1951 is one plausible reason for a change in the relationship. It appears from the chart that there was a major change during the following year, for the observed free-reserve ratios were larger than the predicted in most months before April, 1952.

INFLUENCE OF THE EXCESS PROFITS TAX IN 1952 AND 1953

From mid-1952 to mid-1953 the actual free-reserve ratios were much lower than would have been predicted from the average relationship for the whole 1947–58 period. One possible explanation for this is that the excess profits tax in effect in those years provided a special incentive for banks to borrow. Under the Excess Profits Tax of 1950—which was applied to taxable years that ended after June 30, 1950, and began before January 1, 1954—up to 75 per cent of borrowed capital could be taken into account in computing exemptions from the tax.[7] Member-bank borrowing from the Federal Reserve came within the definition of borrowed capital, although bank deposits did not. For some banks with earnings subject to the tax, borrowing from the Federal Reserve could produce a tax saving equivalent to an aftertax yield of 2.7 per cent on the borrowed funds.[8] A Federal Reserve survey found that only one-fifth to one-quarter of insured commercial banks had earnings subject to the excess profits tax in 1951.[9] Nevertheless in December, 1952, total member-bank borrowing rose rapidly to a peak that has not been equaled since. Federal Reserve authorities recognized that part of the member-bank borrowing in 1952 and 1953 was attributable to efforts of banks to reduce their tax liability; and so the revision of Regulation A in February, 1955, excluded borrowing for tax advantage from the list of appropriate uses of discounting.[10] The 1952–53 episode can be looked upon as evidence that member-bank borrowing is responsive to changes in the spread between yields on earning assets and the cost of borrowed funds.

TESTS OF THE PERIOD JANUARY, 1954, THROUGH DECEMBER, 1959

Because of the evidence of structural shifts discussed above, the 1954–59 period was selected for further testing. As with the earlier tests, the influence of the discount rate could not be estimated when it was introduced as an independent variable. When the discount rate was introduced in the ratio with the bill rate, however, the regression coefficient of the

[7] U.S. 1939 Internal Revenue Code, Excess Profits Taxes, secs. 430, 431, 434, 436, and 437; and *Annual Report of the Secretary of the Treasury on the State of the Finances, for the Fiscal Year Ended June 30, 1951* (Treasury Department Document, No. 3177 [Washington, D.C.: United States Government Printing Office, 1952]), pp. 47–50.

[8] For a sample calculation, assume that a bank was in the 12 per cent excess-profits-tax bracket and had some earnings subject to the tax. Assume also that the proceeds of the extra borrowings were invested in Treasury bills, producing no pretax profit. If the bank had daily-average borrowings of $1 million during the year, $750,000 could be added to the bank's capital base. The bank could then take an excess-profits-tax credit amounting to 12 per cent of the $750,000, or $90,000. The $90,000 could be deducted from the earnings subject to the 30 per cent excess profits tax. For each $1 million borrowed, therefore, net aftertax income could be increased by $27,000, producing a 2.7 per cent aftertax yield on the borrowed funds. This example was suggested by George Coleman, economist of the Mercantile Trust Company, St. Louis.

[9] "Excess Profits Taxes of Commercial Banks," *Federal Reserve Bulletin*, XXXVIII (June, 1952), 602–19.

[10] *Forty-fourth Annual Report of the Board of Governors of the Federal Reserve System, Covering Operations for the Year 1957*, pp. 9–10.

ratio was significant at the 1 per cent level, in equation (T27). The coefficient of multiple determination (R^2) was 0.69.

$$100 \left(\frac{R_F}{D}\right)_t = \underset{(0.0184)}{0.868} - \underset{(0.140)}{0.440} \left(\frac{r_b}{r_d}\right)_{t-1}$$
$$- \underset{(0.0331)}{0.164} \ (r_{3-5})_{t-1} + \underset{(0.0217)}{0.0671} \left(\frac{\phi_{t-1} + \phi_{t-2}}{2}\right). \tag{T27}$$

A simpler equation produced slightly better results, as evidenced by a coefficient of multiple determination of 0.715.

$$100 \left(\frac{R_F}{D}\right)_t = \underset{(0.0163)}{0.508} - \underset{(0.0168)}{0.228} \ (r_b)_t$$
$$+ \underset{(0.0185)}{0.0675} \left(\frac{\phi_{t-1} + \phi_{t-2}}{2}\right). \tag{T35}$$

When the predicted and actual free-reserve ratios were plotted with respect to time, as in the left-hand panel of Figure 13, there was evidence of serial correlation of the residuals again. Two hypotheses were then investigated through use of scatter diagrams. The first was that a linear regression might not be a good enough approximation of the actual relationship among the variables. According to the theory developed in chapter iv, the relationship could be expected to be curvilinear. Furthermore, several regressions in which reciprocals of the interest rates were used had higher coefficients of determination than did any of the linear equations for the period January, 1954, through December, 1959.[11] The other hypothesis was that seasonal variation in the banks' demand for free reserves might account for some of the residual variation.

In Figure 14, the dependent variable, $100 \ (R_F/D)_t$, was adjusted for the deviations from the means of the ϕ term of equation (T35) and a scatter diagram was plotted of the adjusted values and the Treasury bill rate.[12] This was done in order to show the relation between variations in bill rate and variations in the free-reserve ratio, after variation associated with the rate of change of unborrowed reserves, ϕ, had been eliminated. Let

$$z = \frac{\phi_{t-1} + \phi_{t-2}}{2}.$$

[11] See equations (T31), (T32), (T33), and (T34) in Appendix C.

[12] The method used was adapted from one prescribed by Ezekiel and Fox for determining partial regression curves graphically (Mordecai Ezekiel and Karl A. Fox, *Methods of Correlation and Regression Analysis, Linear and Curvilinear* [3d ed.; New York: John Wiley & Sons, Inc., 1959], pp. 210–48).

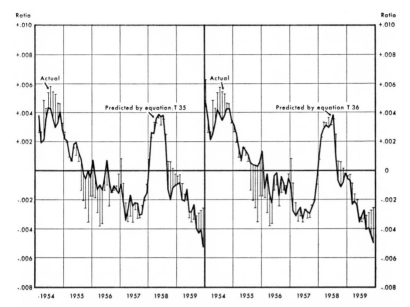

FIG. 13.—Actual free-reserve ratios and ratios predicted by equations (T35) and (T36). Regression equation (T35) in the left-hand panel was fitted to data for February, 1954, through December, 1959. The coefficient of multiple determination, R^2, was 0.76.

$$100 \left(\frac{R_F}{D}\right)_t = \begin{array}{c} 0.508 \\ (0.0163) \end{array} - \begin{array}{c} 0.228(r_b)_t \\ (0.0168) \end{array}$$
$$+ \begin{array}{c} 0.0675 \\ (0.0185) \end{array} \left(\frac{\phi_{t-1} + \phi_{t-2}}{2}\right). \tag{T35}$$

and

$$\phi = \frac{1}{R_U}\frac{dR_U}{dt} - \frac{D}{R_U}\frac{d(R_R/D)}{dt}.$$

Regression equation (T36) was fitted to data for January, 1954, through December, 1959. It included a proxy seasonal variable for each month of the year that could have values of 0 or 1, on the assumption that seasonal variation in the member banks' demand for free reserves was additive and independent of the other variables. It had a coefficient of multiple determination, R^2, of 0.91.

$$100 \left(\frac{R_F}{D}\right)_t =$$
$$-0.251(r_b)_t + 0.047\phi_{t-1} + 0.606S_1 + 0.628S_2$$
$$+0.558S_3 \quad +0.518S_4 \quad +0.476S_5 + 0.534S_6 \tag{T36}$$
$$+0.503S_7 \quad +0.540S_8 \quad +0.630S_9 + 0.611S_{10}$$
$$+0.579S_{11} \quad +0.676S_{12}.$$

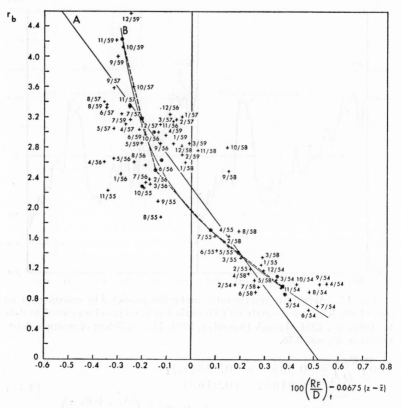

FIG. 14.—Scatter diagram of bill rate and free-reserve ratio adjusted to rate of change of unborrowed reserves, and first approximation curve fitted to the averages. The equation for the net regression line A for the free-reserve ratio on the bill rate (derived from equation T35) is:

$$\left[100 \left(\frac{R_F}{D} \right)_t - 0.0675 (z - \bar{z}) \right] = 0.521 - 0.228 \, r_b. \quad (5.7)$$

The residuals obtained by subtracting free-reserve ratios predicted by equation (T35) from the actual ratios were then plotted with respect to the net regression line, according to the method prescribed by Ezekiel and Fox, *Methods of Correlation and Regression Analysis* . . . , pp. 210–48. Encircled points are averages of points within selected ranges of the bill rate.

$$z = \frac{\phi_{t-1} + \phi_{t-2}}{2},$$

and

$$\phi = \frac{1}{R_U} \frac{dR_U}{dt} - \frac{D}{R_U} \frac{d(R_R / D)}{dt}.$$

Then

$$100 \left(\frac{R_F}{D}\right)_t = 0.508 - 0.228\,(r_b)_t + 0.0675\,z\,. \quad \text{(T35)}$$

The equation of the net regression line (A) showing the change in 100 $(R_F/D)_t$ with changes in the bill rate, while holding the rate of change of unborrowed reserves term, z, constant, is:

$$\left[100 \left(\frac{R_F}{D}\right)_t - 0.0675\,(z - \bar z) \right]$$

$$= 0.508 + 0.0675\,\bar z - 0.228\,r_b\,, \quad (5.6)$$

and

$$\left[100 \left(\frac{R_F}{D}\right)_t - 0.0675\,(z - \bar z) \right] = 0.521 - 0.228\,r_b\,. \quad (5.7)$$

The difference between the actual value of the free-reserve ratio and the value estimated by equation (T35) for each observation was then used to locate a point with respect to the net regression line, with the respective value of the bill rate as the ordinate. A freehand curve was drawn through group averages of the points.

If the dates of the points are examined, it appears that a considerable proportion of the Octobers, Novembers, Decembers, Januarys, and Februarys fall to the right of the net regression line, indicating that in those months the banks tended to maintain larger free-reserve ratios than would be predicted by the average relationship with the bill rate. A marked seasonal distribution of points appears also in Figure 15, where the net regression for the free-reserve ratio on the rate of change of unborrowed reserves is plotted with the bill rate held constant.

It was assumed that the seasonal variation was additive and independent of the other variables, for a first approximation. A regression equation including a proxy seasonal variable for each month of the year was then fitted to the data. The seasonal variable for a given month, S_1 in January, for example, was assumed to be equal to 1 during that month and to be equal to 0 all the rest of the time.[13] The regression equation was:

$$100 \left(\frac{R_F}{D}\right)_t = -0.251\,(r_b)_t + 0.047\,\phi_{t-1} + 0.606\,S_1 + 0.628\,S_2$$
$$+ 0.558\,S_3 + 0.518\,S_4 + 0.476\,S_5 + 0.534\,S_6 \quad \text{(T36)}$$
$$+ 0.503\,S_7 + 0.540\,S_8 + 0.630\,S_9 + 0.611\,S_{10}$$
$$+ 0.579\,S_{11} + 0.676\,S_{12}\,.$$

The coefficient of multiple determination, R^2, was 0.91.

[13] The approach was adapted from a method for treating seasonal variation presented by Lawrence R. Klein, *A Textbook of Econometrics* (Evanston, Illinois: Row, Peterson and Company, 1956), pp. 313–22.

The possibility that the relationship is curvilinear does not appear to be so clearly indicated after seasonal variation has been allowed for, as can be seen from Figure 16. The distribution of the points suggested that there must have been another structural shift, since points for 1954 through mid-1956 lie predominantly to the left of the net regression line while most of the points for later dates fall to the right. When the points are separated into two groups, with all points from January, 1954, through

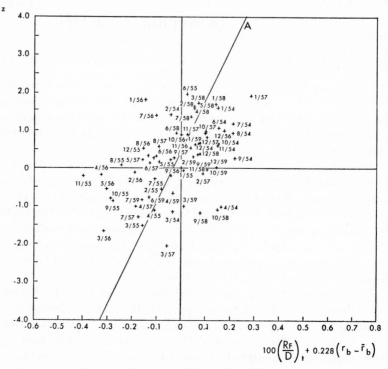

$$100\left(\frac{R_F}{D}\right)_t + 0.228\left(r_b - \bar{r}_b\right)$$

Fig. 15.—Scatter diagram of rate of change of unborrowed reserves and free-reserve ratio adjusted to the bill rate. The net regression equation for the free-reserve ratio on the rate of change of unborrowed reserves (derived from equation T35) is:

$$\left[100\left(\frac{R_F}{D}\right)_t + 0.228\left(r_b - \bar{r}_b\right)\right] = -0.023 + 0.0675z \qquad (5.8)$$

$$z = \frac{\phi_{t-1} + \phi_{t-2}}{2}$$

$$\phi = \frac{1}{R_U}\frac{dR_U}{dt} - \frac{D}{R_U}\frac{d(R_R/D)}{dt}.$$

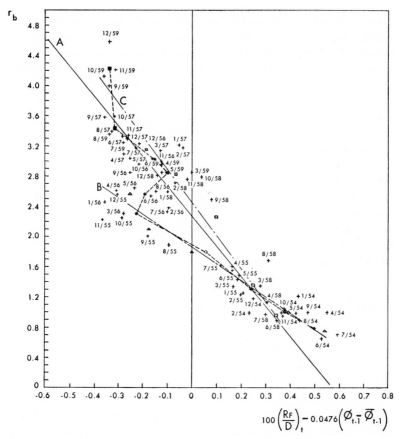

$$100 \left(\frac{R_F}{D}\right)_t - 0.0476\left(\overline{\varnothing}_{t\text{-}1} - \overline{\varnothing}_{t\text{-}1}\right)$$

FIG. 16.—Scatter diagram of bill rate and free-reserve ratio adjusted to rate of change of unborrowed reserves and seasonal coefficients. The equation for the net regression line A for the free-reserve ratio on the bill rate (derived from equation T36) is:

$$\left[100 \left(\frac{R_F}{D}\right)_t - 0.476(\phi_{t-1} - \bar{\phi}_{t-1})\right] = 0.572 - 0.251 \, (r_b)_t . \quad (5.9)$$

The procedure followed was the same as for Figures 14 and 15. Encircled points are averages of the points within selected ranges of the bill rate when all of the points for January, 1954, through December, 1959, are taken into consideration. Points indicated by triangles are averages of points for the period January, 1954, through June, 1956, within selected ranges of the bill rate. Points indicated by squares are averages of the points for the period after June, 1956. The lines B and C approximating the relationships for the subperiods have been fitted by eye.

June, 1956, in one group and all later points in another, it appears that the relationship of the free-reserve ratio and the bill rate was distinctly different in the two periods and might be approximated by a linear function in either case. Curvilinearity has not been ruled out; the evidence of these tests is insufficient to establish it, however. The periods were judged to be too short to justify fitting multiple regression equations for them separately by the method of least squares.

Although equation (T36) is not satisfactory for estimating the parameters of the free-reserves demand function, an estimating equation can be drawn from it that might be useful for Federal Reserve operating purposes, despite the apparent shift in the relationships that occurred between 1954 and 1959. Taking the slope of the net regression line for the latest period, line C, as the regression coefficient for the bill rate (estimated graphically), and using the seasonal coefficients and the regression coefficient for the rate of change of unborrowed reserves estimated over the whole 1954–59 period, would produce the following estimating equation, which actually is very little different from (T36):

$$
\begin{aligned}
100 \left(\frac{R_F}{D}\right)_t = &- 0.23\,(r_b)_t + 0.047\,\phi_{t-1} + 0.60\,S_1 + 0.62\,S_2 \\
&+ 0.55\,S_3 \ \ + 0.51\,S_4 \ \ \ + 0.47\,S_5 + 0.52\,S_6 \quad (5.10) \\
&+ 0.49\,S_7 \ \ + 0.53\,S_8 \ \ \ + 0.62\,S_9 + 0.60\,S_{10} \\
&+ 0.57\,S_{11} \ + 0.67\,S_{12}\,.
\end{aligned}
$$

Equation (5.10) could be used to predict the free-reserve ratio each month for use in a statistical control chart. Comparing the actual free-reserve ratios with the predicted ratios on the chart would then aid in the early detection of shifts in the banks' demand for free reserves, which would influence the quantity of reserves that would have to be provided by the Federal Reserve in order to produce a desired change in member-bank deposits. As experience accumulates, the estimating equation could be revised.

POSSIBLE EXPLANATIONS FOR A SHIFT IN THE FREE
RESERVES-INTEREST RELATIONSHIP

The period January, 1954, through December, 1959, included two periods in which the free-reserve ratio was predominantly negative—mid-1955 through the end of 1957, and September, 1958, through the end of 1959. In the first of these periods the observed free-reserve ratios tended to be lower than the predicted, and in the second period observed free-reserve ratios were higher than would be predicted by the average relationship of free-reserve ratios to bill rates. This could be considered evidence that the free reserves-interest relationship is not a stable one. There is some evidence, however, to support a hypothesis that the banks' demand schedules for free reserves were shifted as the result of changes in other conditions—specifically, a change in administration of the discount window by the Reserve Banks.

The discount mechanism had been little used from 1934 until 1952, when borrowing rose rapidly. According to the Board of Governors, "During this initial revival of the discount mechanism after a generation of disuse numerous problems arose, including uncertainty among many member banks about what was an appropriate use of the discount privilege."[14] The revised Regulation A set out general rules in February, 1955. The individual Reserve Banks, however, had to work out detailed criteria and procedures for administering borrowing in the light of special conditions in their respective districts. Furthermore, the task of informing the member banks regarding the limits applicable to them required time, since the limits were determined to some extent on a case-by-case basis, and banks found to be making inappropriate use of the borrowing privilege were (and are) generally given time to make required portfolio adjustments gradually. Therefore, it seems reasonable to expect that the volume of member-bank borrowing at any given interest rate would be smaller in 1959 than in 1955 and 1956, because of an increase in effectiveness of discount administration.[15] This is not to say that the Federal Reserve Banks vary the restrictiveness of administering the window contracyclically. It merely implies that the effectiveness of regulation and the attitudes of the member banks toward regulation have changed over time.

The implied change, if it has occurred, is equivalent to an increase in the actual discount rate, as distinguished from the nominal discount rate used in some of the regressions of this study. A possible way to test for the influence of changes in administration of discounting would be to cor-

[14] *Annual Report Covering Operations for the Year 1957*, p. 9.

[15] Charles R. Whittlesey maintains that some Federal Reserve Banks have the reputation of being stricter than others in the enforcement of Regulation A, but that such differences among the Reserve Banks appear to have diminished in recent years. He also cites the experience of a Reserve Bank that brought about a marked reduction of borrowing in its district through an educational program to explain to bankers the System's attitude toward borrowing. Whittlesey, *Quarterly Journal of Economics*, LXXIII (May, 1959), 211, 214. See also Robert Roosa's "Comment . . . ," *ibid.*, pp. 333–37. In part to increase member-bank understanding of discount administration, Federal Reserve Banks treated the subject in their monthly publications during 1959; for example, Federal Reserve Bank of Philadelphia, *Business Review*, January, 1959, pp. 16–26; and Federal Reserve Bank of New York, *Monthly Review*, September, 1959, pp. 138–42.

relate interest rates with ratios of borrowings to deposits for the individual Federal Reserve districts. Differences in timing of shifts in the relationships from district to district might indicate changes in discount policy at particular Reserve Banks. Such tests, however, were considered to be outside the scope of this study.

Member-bank demand for excess reserves also appears to have shifted. In 1954 the free-reserve ratio was higher than would be predicted by the average relationship, although in 1958 it was not. Development of the Federal funds market over the period may have reduced the volume of excess reserves the banks want to hold at any given interest rate.

SOME IMPLICATIONS OF TIME LAGS FOR THE DIRECTION OF CAUSATION IN THE FREE RESERVES-INTEREST RELATIONSHIP

The evidence considered here indicates that the desired free-reserve ratio of the member banks is functionally related to market interest rates. The scatter diagrams with annual data and all of the regressions with monthly data suggest that market interest rates—the Treasury bill rate in particular—have a strong influence upon the free-reserve ratio. The influence of the discount rate has not been clearly identified, although some of the tests indicate that it has effects on free reserves in the direction predicted by the hypothesis.

An alternative hypothesis—part of the reserve position theory discussed in chapter ii—would attribute the observed correlations not to the influence of interest rates upon the desired free-reserve ratios of banks but instead to the influence of free-reserve ratios upon interest rates. If it could be found that changes in interest rates typically preceded changes in the free-reserve ratio, or vice versa, this observation would strengthen the argument for accepting one hypothesis rather than the other. A systematic investigation of time lags was not made in this study, but some evidence on the significance of lagging certain of the variables was turned up incidentally.

In the few instances in which interest rates were used in regressions with a lag, there was no indication that the correlation with the free-reserve ratio was improved. However, the shortest lag used was a full month, which might exceed the typical reaction time of the banking system. George Horwich and Robert P. Black have concluded from their studies that the responses of banks to changes in their stock of reserves usually occur within less than one month. Robert C. Turner, in his study of member-bank borrowing for 1922 through 1936, found that changes in the spread between discount rates and market rates tended to be synchronous with changes in borrowing or to precede changes in borrowing, with the movements being most closely synchronized in the New York, Chicago, and Boston Federal Reserve districts.[16]

Open-Market Operations and the Free-Reserve Ratio

Open-market operations, as indicated by the rate of change of unborrowed reserves, apparently exerted relatively little influence on the free-reserve ratio in the years 1947 through 1959. The indicated influence of market interest rates was much greater. The beta coefficient of the bill rate in equation (T35), for example, was -0.806, as compared with a beta weight of 0.271 for ϕ, the rate of change of unborrowed reserves adjusted for changes in the required-reserves ratio. Furthermore, open-market operations appeared to affect the free-reserves ratio with a time lag; the influence of ϕ was sharply increased by introducing it in the regression equations with a lead of a month or two.

The evidence that the influence of open-market operations upon the free-reserve ratio was small is consistent with the hypotheses of this study but tends to contradict a key hypothesis of the reserve position doctrine discussed earlier. According to reserve position doctrine, the Federal Reserve controls member-bank borrowing or free reserves through use of open-market operations, although market interest rates or credit demands may also have some influence. Otherwise, there would be no reason for considering member-bank borrowing or free reserves as proximate objectives of open-market operations.

The evidence presented here might, however, be interpreted to mean merely that the Federal Reserve did not in fact exert much influence upon the free-reserve ratio in the observed period. Whether or not open-market operations could have had more influence upon the free-reserve ratio cannot be determined from the evidence of this study. By the theory of chapter iv, open-market operations and interest rates both influence the free-reserve ratio, and so the Federal Reserve might be able to offset the influence of interest rate changes through changing the rate at which it provides or withdraws unborrowed reserves.

Time Lags in the Influence of Open-Market Operations upon Free Reserves

At first thought, the evidence that open-market operations affect the free-reserve ratio with a time lag might seem implausible. In the usual blackboard demonstration of Federal Reserve open-market operations, a

---

[16] Turner, *Member-Bank Borrowing*, pp. 96–144.

purchase of $10 million in securities by the Federal Reserve is reflected immediately in the member-bank T-accounts as an increase in deposits on one side and as an increase in total reserves, distributed between excess reserves and required reserves, on the other. Although the effect of a single open-market purchase upon excess reserves is instantaneous, it may be short-lived; the banks affected might partially or entirely offset it on the following day. If many successive transactions of the Federal Reserve and the banks are summed into net rates of change or flow over time, lags in the effects of open-market operations upon daily-average stock measures of excess reserves and borrowing can be explained. Two possible explanations are presented here as suggestions for future studies, one in terms of the adjustment processes of the banking system and one in terms of interest rate effects.

In chapter iv, it was argued that when open-market operations increase the rate of growth of unborrowed reserves, with interest rates remaining constant, the rate of deposit expansion and the free-reserve ratio increase for a time. The change in open-market operations has an immediate effect upon the *rate of change* of the free-reserve ratio, but some time is required for a change in the average *level* to take place because the banks will in effect be resisting the change by buying assets. Assuming the rate of growth of unborrowed reserves remains constant at a new higher rate, eventually the free-reserve ratio will reach a level at which the banks' efforts to reduce it by buying assets are exactly offset by the rate at which open-market operations supply additional unborrowed reserves. During the period of adjustment the rate of deposit expansion in percentage terms is less than the rate of growth of unborrowed reserves because some of the additional reserves are used by the banks to repay borrowings and to increase excess reserves in raising the free-reserve ratio. When the adjustment has been completed the free-reserve ratio is higher than it was initially and the percentage rate of deposit expansion is equal to the rate of growth of unborrowed reserves. The characteristic lag of the monthly rate of deposit expansion behind the rate of change of unborrowed reserves revealed in Figure 3 is consistent with the view that changes in the free-reserve ratio absorb or release reserves when open-market operations change the rate of growth of unborrowed reserves.

There is no way of judging from the hypotheses whether the average adjustment period is a matter of days or weeks. The evidence supplied by the multiple regressions suggests that the adjustment period may be more than a month. The rate of change of unborrowed reserves was found to be the principal influence determining the rate of change of the free-reserve ratio, in multiple regressions for 1947 through 1958.[17] Thus, when the rate of growth of unborrowed reserves increases, the free-reserve ratio apparently begins at once to increase also. As can be seen from Figure 3, however, the rate of change of unborrowed reserves reversed direction nearly every month. Consequently, the free-reserve ratio generally did not have time to adjust completely before the rate of growth or contraction of unborrowed reserves changed again. Evidence of incomplete adjustment in Figure 3 is that the rate of change of deposits almost always fell short of the rate of change of unborrowed reserves in either direction, indicating that some reserves were being absorbed or released by changes in the free-reserve ratio during each month.

In the regression equations, the value of the free-reserve ratio each month reflects, in part, how much it was influenced by open-market operations in the preceding month or months. It appears, therefore, that open-market operations over the 1947–59 period tended to force the banks' free-reserve ratios to one side or the other of their desired positions by small amounts on the average, thus accounting for the relatively small influence of open-market operations as compared to interest rates. Furthermore, the effects of open-market operations were cumulative, accounting for a time lag in the average net effect.

An interest rate explanation for lags in the response of free reserves to open-market operations can be based upon the contention of this study that market interest rates are not determined by the free-reserve ratio but that they are influenced by the rates per unit of time at which the Federal Reserve System and the member banks buy and sell assets. A clue for later investigations might be provided by the following tentative hypothesis: A change in the rate of growth of unborrowed reserves, other conditions remaining the same, induces a change in the rate at which banks buy assets and thus influences market interest rates. Because there are many other influences upon market interest rates and because there is some slippage between the rates of change of unborrowed reserves and bank assets, the relationship between ϕ and interest rates is not a close one and operates with a time lag. The change in interest rates induced by a change in the rate of change of unborrowed reserves then influences the banks to alter the free-reserve ratio, which they do promptly since banks somewhere in the System must make reserve adjustments daily. The rate of change of unborrowed reserves therefore influences the free-reserve ratio not only directly but also through changes of interest rates, thus accounting for the time lag.

No attempt was made to estimate a relationship between the rate of

[17] See equations (T10–12) in Appendix B.

change of unborrowed reserves and market interest rates but a few coefficients of simple correlation between ϕ and the bill rate with various time lags were produced in the course of estimating the multiple regressions, and these were at least consistent in direction with the tentative hypothesis above. For January, 1954, through December, 1959, the coefficient of simple correlation for ϕ and the contemporaneous bill rate was -0.046, which was not significant. With the bill rate lagging by one month the coefficient of simple correlation was -0.15 which was significant at the 20 per cent level. When the average of ϕ for two preceding months was correlated with the bill rate, the coefficient of correlation was -0.21; significant between the 5 and 10 per cent levels. The slopes of the regression lines were not estimated. There is no intention here of basing much of an argument upon such fragmentary findings. Nevertheless, the evidence is suggestive and might be useful in planning future studies.

VI

Conclusions

FREE RESERVES AS A PROXIMATE OBJECTIVE OF OPEN-MARKET OPERATIONS

THE PURPOSE of a proximate objective, in the sense used here, is to indicate to the Federal Reserve when and by how much open-market operations should add or withdraw reserves in order to induce the member banks to expand or contract deposits at some desired rate. In reserve position doctrine the volume of member-bank free reserves, or of member-bank borrowing in the earlier version, is viewed as an index of the "pressure" applied by the Federal Reserve to the member banks in order to induce or to restrain bank credit expansion. If the Federal Reserve wishes to increase the banks' incentive for buying assets, open-market operations should supply additional reserves rapidly enough to increase member-bank free reserves, according to the doctrine.

Reserve position doctrine has directed attention to variables—member-bank borrowings and excess reserves—that exert a significant influence upon bank behavior. This has been perhaps its main contribution to understanding how the monetary system operates. Unfortunately, as commonly used, the doctrine has had a serious defect: There has been a tendency to interpret equal volumes of free reserves as having approximately equal influence on bank behavior at all times. The principal conclusion of this study is that what really matters is the difference between the *actual* free reserves of the banks and their *desired* free reserves. Because the desired reserve position changes with demand and other conditions, the significance of a given actual reserve position may be very different at one time than at another. Modifying the doctrine by incorporating the concept of a changing desired reserve position increases the explanatory power of the theory and suggests major changes in its application to the control problems of the central bank.

When the concept of a changing desired reserve position is introduced, the use of free reserves as a proximate objective for open-market operations may be questioned on two main grounds: First, although open-market operations do influence the free reserves of the member banks, free reserves in the postwar period examined in this study have been influenced more by movements of interest rates than by open-market operations. In

87

view of the influence of other factors upon the reserve positions of banks, it might be difficult for the central bank to maintain a given level of free reserves through use of open-market operations. Second, there is no one actual volume of free reserves associated with a particular rate of deposit expansion; a wide range of rates of deposit change can occur with a specific free-reserve level under different conditions.

THE LINK BETWEEN OPEN-MARKET OPERATIONS AND MEMBER-BANK RESERVE POSITIONS

There apparently is a tendency for short-run changes in the volume of borrowing or the free-reserve ratio to occur in an offsetting direction when the rate of change of unborrowed reserves changes. It may have been these short-run movements in borrowings that led some early observers to conclude that open-market operations could not control total reserves directly but that they could control member-bank borrowing. Hardy, however, observed that the offsetting changes in discounting of the 1920's were only partial, and concluded that if the Federal Reserve pressed far enough with open-market operations it could achieve a desired change in total member-bank reserves. His description of a hypothetical time sequence of reactions to open-market operations is consistent with the behavior of the mechanism hypothesized in this study.[1]

The originators of reserve position doctrine did not employ multiple regression analysis, so did not hold interest rates constant, in effect, while estimating the relationship between open-market operations and member-bank borrowing. The influence of open-market operations upon borrowing may thus have been over-estimated. In some of the years they observed, it seems plausible that interest rates may have changed enough to produce an apparent inverse correlation between borrowings and Federal Reserve security holdings. In other years, as Harris, Hardy, and Currie pointed out, changes of interest rates and of demand for credit did not occur in such a way as to produce a good correlation.

The early reserve position doctrine argument that open-market operations control member-bank borrowing was reinforced by hypotheses that excluded interest rates as an influence on the volume of borrowing. The doctrine in fact went much further in asserting that the volume of borrowing was the principal determinant of short-term market rates. A correlation between market interest rates and the volume of member-bank borrowing was interpreted by Dr. Riefler, Jan Tinbergen, and others, as we have seen earlier, to be evidence that the volume of member-bank bor-

[1] Beryl W. Sprinkel has presented a description of response lags in the deposit expansion mechanism (*Journal of Finance*, XIV [September, 1959], 341–46).

rowing influences interest rates, The same observed correlation has been interpreted by others as evidence that interest rates influence the volume of borrowing. The inference as to direction of causation in each case must rest upon a priori grounds. The distinctive a priori argument for the Riefler-Tinbergen interpretation is that banks are extremely reluctant to be in debt to the Federal Reserve and that hence a bank will borrow only when forced to by a loss of reserves. The alternative inference is based upon the assumption that banks are profit-maximizing institutions whose behavior with respect to market prices should be similar to behavior of profit-maximizing firms observed in many other markets. Banks, accordingly, would be expected to increase borrowing when a rise of market interest rates in relation to borrowing costs would make it more profitable to do so.

Although the assumption that banks are reluctant to borrow is the key to the Riefler-Tinbergen inference, it is not inconsistent with the opposite interpretation, for reluctance is like many other manifestations of preferences that are amenable to economic analysis. Reluctance to borrow may influence banks' demand for borrowing without making the banks indifferent to interest rate changes. Polakoff, for example, has demonstrated through use of indifference curves how banks' reluctance to borrow would be expected to influence the shape of the banks' demand schedule for borrowed reserves.[2]

The tradition against borrowing might be more properly described as a tradition against continuous borrowing by any one bank. An increase in aggregate member-bank borrowing in response to an increase in market interest rates (in relation to borrowing costs) does not require that any bank become continuously indebted to the Federal Reserve, nor does it require that all member banks borrow. Daily-average borrowing can rise through an increase in the number of banks making temporary use of the discount window for daily adjustments, without any banks violating the tradition against continuous borrowing or making improper use of the borrowing privilege as defined by Regulation A.

The hypothesis that member-bank borrowing is not responsive to changes in market interest rates cannot be confirmed solely by demonstrating that banks are reluctant to borrow; the characteristics of the demand schedule must be determined by direct empirical observation of borrowing and interest rates. The empirical evidence produced by this study and others indicates that aggregate member-bank borrowing is indeed influenced by the net yields obtainable on borrowed funds, within a considerable part of the range of interest rates and other conditions

[2] Polakoff, *Journal of Finance*, XV (March, 1960), 1–18.

observed. The efforts of the Federal Reserve Banks to control the volume of member-bank borrowing through administrative means, which have extended through much of the System's history, are also evidence that at times banks must have been influenced by the profitability of borrowing. Had they not been, there should have been less necessity for restraining them.

The evidence of this study that the monthly-average free-reserve ratios of the member banks in the postwar period were influenced more by interest rates than by the rate of change of unborrowed reserves (representing open-market operations) does not necessarily mean that the Federal Reserve could not control bank reserve positions if it wanted to do so.[3] The hypotheses and evidence of this study do indicate, however, that open-market operations would have to supply reserves at a greater rate in order to produce a given free-reserve level under some conditions than under others. The rate required would depend upon what the desired reserve position of the banks would be under the prevailing conditions.

The Link between Reserve Positions and the Rate of Deposit Expansion

The proposition that different rates of change of unborrowed reserves would be required at different times in order to keep the free reserves of the banks at a specific level has important implications for the control of deposit expansion. Suppose, for purposes of illustration, that the Federal Reserve decides for some reason to try to maintain a level of $500 million net borrowed reserves through use of open-market operations. Suppose further that member-bank deposits and member-bank credit are expanding at a rate judged to be satisfactory. If market interest rates then decline, the banks' choices between borrowing from the Federal Reserve or selling assets in order to meet reserve losses are tipped toward selling assets; the cost in asset yields foregone has declined in comparison to the cost of borrowing. Banks then begin paying off their borrowings at the Federal Reserve, selling assets in order to do so. Each time the banks succeed in reducing borrowings and/or increasing excess reserves by a perceptible amount the change in net borrowed reserves would be taken by the Federal Reserve as a signal to withdraw some reserves through open-market operations, in order to restore net borrowed reserves to the target

---

[3] In estimating the influence of open-market operations on the free-reserve ratio by the methods used here, it is not necessary to assume that the Federal Reserve was attempting to control member-bank free reserves during the period examined. Whatever the Federal Reserve's objectives happened to be, open-market operations were a measurable influence upon the free-reserve ratio and upon the rate of deposit expansion.

level. The immediate effect of each open-market withdrawal of reserves is to make the banks' net borrowed reserves greater than the banks want them to be, inducing another round of asset sales by the banks, and so on.

If the net borrowed reserves target is not changed, a decline in market interest rates therefore has the following consequences:

1. The desired reserve position of the banks changes, inducing banks to attempt to reduce their indebtedness to the Federal Reserve and/or to increase excess reserves.

2. Open-market operations withdraw reserves to offset the banks' efforts to change their reserve position.

3. Deposits contract (or the rate of expansion diminishes).

The point of the illustration is that if a fixed free or net borrowed reserve level were to be adopted as a proximate objective of open-market operations ‚ the rate of change of unborrowed reserves (open-market operations) and the rate of deposit expansion or contraction would both then be determined by the banks' demand for excess reserves and borrowings. If the banks want to increase their free reserves and if the Federal Reserve frustrates their attempts by withdrawing reserves, deposits contract or the rate of expansion is reduced. If the banks want to reduce their free reserves and if the Federal Reserve frustrates their attempts by injecting additional reserves, deposits expand. Thus, open-market operations in effect influence the free reserves of the member banks by changing the rate of deposit expansion or contraction.

Fluctuations in member-bank demands for free reserves have implications for deposit expansion rates in seasonal, cyclical, and secular contexts. For example, some of the tests of this study indicate that banks prefer to hold larger free reserves at any given combination of interest rates in some months of the year than in others. Consequently, a policy of attempting to maintain a constant level of free reserves over the year would produce seasonal variation in rates of change of unborrowed reserves and member-bank deposits. Similarly, if the Federal Reserve were to attempt to maintain a given level of net borrowed reserves as a restraining measure during a boom, the onset of a cyclical contraction in business activity might induce a contraction in member-bank deposits and money supply before it became evident that the need for restriction had passed. Over longer periods of time, a policy of attempting to maintain net borrowed reserves at $500 million, for example, might be expected to be more restrictive in its effects on deposit expansion in some years than in others.

It is not argued here that the Federal Reserve sets free or net borrowed reserves targets and then tries to maintain them in the inflexible manner described here for purposes of illustration. Open-market operations have only to delay the member banks' attempts to change reserve positions, however, in order to produce some of the effects on deposit expansion rates described above. If open-market operations tend to stabilize free or net borrowed reserve levels, or to slow their movement, as they indeed appear to do, the rate of deposit expansion must then be determined in part by changes in the demand for bank credit. It may be argued that this is desirable; that bank credit and money supply should expand when demand for them increases and contract when demand contracts. Such an argument, however, is part of a discussion of the more ultimate objectives of monetary policy and is outside the scope of this study.

Use of Total Reserves or Unborrowed Reserves as a Guide

Reserve position doctrine, as modified by incorporating the concept of a changing desired reserve position, supplies a theoretical explanation of the reasons banks expand or contract deposits in response to open-market operations of the Federal Reserve and to changes in credit demands and interest rates. It suggests, furthermore, a way of organizing an approach to the problem of using the rates of change of unborrowed reserves or total reserves as proximate objectives of open-market operations. According to an accounting relationship that underlies Figure 3, the percentage rate of change of member-bank deposits is equal to the rate of change of unborrowed reserves except when the reserve-requirement ratio and the free-reserve ratio are changing.

Assuming that Federal Reserve open-market operations can control the rate of change of unborrowed reserves, the theory would be complete if behavior of the reserve ratios could be predicted. No attempt was made in this study to explain the behavior of the reserve-requirement ratio. Experiments conducted in the course of the study indicated that actual behavior of the free-reserve ratio in the postwar period was consistent with the hypotheses presented in chapter iv. Evidence can be found in other studies and for other periods that is also consistent with the hypotheses. The free-reserve ratio, therefore, does behave in a predictable way. Additional research may increase ability to predict the free-reserve ratio.

The gist of the modified reserve position theory is that banks seek to maintain certain desired ratios of excess reserves and borrowings, or free reserves, to total deposits. These desired ratios are related to market interest rates, the discount rate, expected deposit movements, and possibly other variables, such as the relative proportions of assets of varying yields and riskiness in bank portfolios. When actual free-reserve ratios differ from the desired reserve ratios, because of changes in the stock of unborrowed reserves or in any of the variables influencing the desired reserve ratios, the banks attempt to adjust by buying or selling assets and borrowing or repaying indebtedness at the Federal Reserve Banks, thus causing total deposits to change. The Federal Reserve could conceivably produce any desired rate of change of deposits by controlling the rate of change of unborrowed reserves and by allowing for expected changes in the free-reserve ratio in advance, or by making adjustments to them as they occur. Allowance could also be made for reserve-requirement changes.

There are some built-in sources of instability in the deposit expansion mechanism, as it is now constituted, such as the ability of banks to vary their excess reserves and their borrowings and a tendency for aggregate reserve requirements to change because of differences in the reserve requirements applied to various classes of deposits. One approach to these sources of instability might be to reduce their influence through institutional changes, by eliminating member-bank borrowing or instituting uniform reserve requirements, for example. The other, of course, is to learn to cope with them by becoming more familiar with their behavior.

There obviously is much more to be learned about the characteristics of the mechanism described here. The experiments of this study merely scratched the surface of the possibilities that might be investigated. One of the most interesting subjects for future exploration would be the various time lags of the mechanism. Another interesting problem would be to determine the significance of changing regional distributions of deposits. And beyond the problem of mastering the management of member-bank deposits lies the problem of extending the theory to prediction of the rate of growth of the total money supply.

Interpreting the Federal Reserve Statement

Friday morning press reports of the Federal Reserve's weekly statement of member-bank reserves and borrowings are usually headed "Net Reserves Fell (or Rose) $XX,000,000 during Week at Member Banks" or "Lending Capacity of Nation's Banks Fell (or Rose) Last Week." Although the sophisticated reader can find much more in the accompanying comments and tables, there is little doubt that many an appraisal of current monetary policy is dominated by the weekly estimate of free or net borrowed reserves. People with investment decisions to make are interested more in future conditions in the money and capital markets than in what has just happened; the free-reserve figure, when taken as a simple indicator of banks' readiness or capacity to lend and invest, has great appeal as a window into the next week. As a clue to Federal Reserve intentions, the free-reserve estimate is perhaps even more popular.

The arguments of this study that question the value of free or net borrowed reserves as a control objective for the Federal Reserve apply also in questioning its value to outside observers. An increase in free reserves may occur with a deliberate or unintentional easing of restrictiveness by the Federal Reserve. At some other time, however, an increase in free reserves may occur when banks actually have been induced to contract credit and deposits. In neither situation can the outside observer deduce from the level of free reserves what the Federal Reserve wants the banks to do or what they are doing. This does not mean that excess reserves and borrowings do not influence bank behavior; it merely means that there are so many other influences at work that the absolute levels of excess reserves and borrowings cannot be depended upon for predictions.

Appendixes

APPENDIX A

REGRESSION EQUATIONS FOR ESTIMATING MONTHLY RATES OF CHANGE OF DEPOSITS AND REQUIRED RESERVES

(Brackets contain coefficients of partial determination, the coefficients of partial correlation squared.)

Equation Number	Period	Regression Equation	Coefficient of Multiple Determination, R^2
T1	Jan., 1947—Dec., 1958	$(1/D)(dD/dt) = 0.471 + 0.0408\,R_F/R - 0.332\,r_b/r_a$	0.104
T2	Jan., 1947—Dec., 1958	$(1/D)(dD/dt) = 0.381 + 0.0390\,R_F/R - 0.0710\,r_a \quad -0.0324\,r_b$	0.104
T3	July, 1951—Dec., 1958	$(1/D)(dD/dt) = 0.00486 + 0.0796\,R_F/R + 0.223\,r_b/r_a$	0.174
T4	July, 1951—Dec., 1958	$(1/D)(dD/dt) = -0.127 + 0.215\,r_b/r_a + 0.111\,R_B/R \quad -0.717\,R_B/R$	0.176
T5	July, 1951—Dec., 1958	$[1/(D-F)][d(D-F)/dt] = 0.876 - 0.879\,(r_b/r_a)_1 - 1.531\,(r_b/r_a)_2 - 1.146\,(r_b/r_a)_3 - 0.885\,(r_b/r_a)_4 - 0.749\,(r_b/r_a)_5 - 0.373\,(r_b/r_a)_6 - 0.361\,(r_b/r_a)_7 - 0.571\,(r_b/r_a)_8 - 0.489\,(r_b/r_a)_9 - 0.259\,(r_b/r_a)_{10} - 0.151\,(r_b/r_a)_{11} - 0.171\,(r_b/r_a)_{12} + 24.2\,R_F/D$	0.543
T6	July, 1951—Dec., 1958	$(1/R_B)(dR_B/dt) = -0.546 + 0.372\,(r_b/r_a)_1 - 0.649\,(r_b/r_a)_2 - 0.189\,(r_b/r_a)_3 + 0.206\,(r_b/r_a)_4 + 0.450\,(r_b/r_a)_5 + 0.828\,(r_b/r_a)_6 + 0.493\,(r_b/r_a)_7 + 0.193\,(r_b/r_a)_8 + 0.741\,(r_b/r_a)_9 + 1.270\,(r_b/r_a)_{10} + 1.483\,(r_b/r_a)_{11} + 1.447\,(r_b/r_a)_{12} + 1.00\,R_F/D$	0.488

APPENDIX A—*Continued*

Equation Number	Period	Regression Equation	Coefficient of Multiple Determination, R^2
T7	Jan., 1947—Dec., 1958	$(1/D)(dD/dt) = 0.588 - 0.679\,(r_b/r_a)_1 - 0.986\,(r_b/r_a)_2 - 0.820\,(r_b/r_a)_3 - 0.704\,(r_b/r_a)_4$ $[0.0607]\ [0.0885]\ [0.0678]\ [0.0540]$ $- 0.615\,(r_b/r_a)_5 - 0.394\,(r_b/r_a)_6 - 0.173\,(r_b/r_a)_7 - 0.191\,(r_b/r_a)_8$ $[0.0428]\ [0.0199]\ [0.0039]\ [0.0049]$ $- 0.182\,(r_b/r_a)_9 - 0.0646\,(r_b/r_a)_{10} + 0.0249\,(r_b/r_a)_{11} - 0.146\,(r_b/r_a)_{12}$ $[0.0049]\ [0.0006]\ [0.0001]\ [0.0031]$ $+ 0.313\,\phi - 0.0470\,R_F/D$ $[0.241]\ [0.0014]$	0.666
T8	Jan., 1947—Dec., 1958	$(1/D)(dD/dt) = 0.275 - 0.138\,(R_F/D)_1 - 0.0962\,(R_F/D)_2 - 0.585\,(R_F/D)_3 - 0.451\,(R_F/D)_4$ $[0.0023]\ [0.0005]\ [0.0267]\ [0.0194]$ $+ 0.102\,(R_F/D)_5 - 0.0442\,(R_F/D)_6 - 0.0328\,(R_F/D)_7 + 0.385\,(R_F/D)_8$ $[0.0007]\ [0.0002]\ [0.0001]\ [0.0127]$ $+ 0.339\,(R_F/D)_9 + 0.197\,(R_F/D)_{10} + 0.0451\,(R_F/D)_{11} + 0.0479\,(R_F/D)_{12}$ $[0.0105]\ [0.0043]\ [0.0002]\ [0.0002]$ $+ 0.456\,\phi - 0.111\,r_b/r_a$ $[0.417]\ [0.0014]$	0.523
T9	Jan., 1947—Dec., 1958	$(1/D)(dD/dt) = 0.175 + 0.489\,\phi - 0.0084\,r_b/r_a - 0.0025\,R_F/D$ $[0.466]\ [0.0000]\ [0.0000]$	0.482

In equations (T1), (T2), (T3), (T4), and (T5), the deposits, D, were seasonally adjusted daily-average member-bank demand deposits less Treasury balances, less demand balances due to domestic banks, and less cash items in process of collection. In the other equations the deposits were daily-average net member-bank demand deposits subject to reserve requirements plus daily-average member-bank time deposits subject to reserve requirements, not seasonally adjusted. Demand balances due to domestic banks and cash items in process of collection were excluded but Treasury balances were not. In equation (T5) Federal Reserve float was deducted from total deposits in the belief that it was a source of random variation in measured deposits.

R_E = monthly daily-average excess reserves.

R_B = monthly daily-average member-bank borrowings from Federal Reserve Banks.

R_F = monthly daily-average free reserves (excess reserves less borrowings).

R_U = monthly daily-average unborrowed reserves.

$(1/D)(dD/dt)$ = monthly per cent change in daily-average deposits.

$(1/R_R)(dR_R/dt)$ = monthly per cent change in monthly daily-average member-bank required reserves.

$\phi = [1/R_U][dR_U/dt] - [D/R_U][d(R_R/D)/dt]$ = monthly per cent change in unborrowed reserves adjusted for changes in reserve requirements.

r_b = monthly average new issue rate on 3-month Treasury bills.

r_d = monthly daily-average New York discount rate.

In equations (T5), (T6), (T7), and (T8), a variable with a number subscript was assumed to be equal to zero except in the month indicated by its subscript.

Sources: J.1 Releases of the Board of Governors of the Federal Reserve System and the *Federal Reserve Bulletin*.

APPENDIX B

REGRESSION EQUATIONS FOR ESTIMATING MONTHLY RATES OF CHANGE OF THE FREE-RESERVE RATIO

(Brackets contain coefficients of partial determination, the coefficients of partial correlation squared.)

Equation Number	Period	Regression Equation	Coefficient of Multiple Determination, R^2
T10	Jan., 1947— Dec., 1958	$100\ d(R_F/D)/dt = -0.0931 + 0.0286\ r_a + 0.0129\ r_b + 0.499\ R_F/D$ $[0.00118]\quad[0.000324]\quad[0.00449]$	0.010
T11	Jan., 1947— Dec., 1958	$100\ d(R_F/D)/dt = -0.011 - 0.0156\ r_a + 0.00936\ r_b - 1.93\ R_F/D + 0.0959\ \phi$ $[0.00113]\quad[0.000548]\quad[0.00213]\quad[0.688]$	0.691
T12	July, 1951— Dec., 1958	$100\ d(R_F^*/D)/dt = -0.626 + 0.0110\ r_a + 0.00278\ r_b - 2.81\ R_F/D + 0.0959\ \phi$ $[0.000561]\quad[0.0000504]\quad[0.00343]\quad[0.659]$	0.667

$d(R_F/D)/dt$ = the change in daily average free-reserve ratio centered on the first of the month to the daily average free-reserve ratio centered on the first of the following month.

r_a = the New York discount rate.

r_b = monthly average new issue yield on Treasury bills.

ϕ = the monthly per cent change in

unborrowed reserves adjusted for changes in the reserve-requirement ratio.

$$\phi = [1/R_U][dR_U/dt] - [D/R_U][d(R_R/D)/dt]$$

Sources: J.1 Releases of the Board of Governors of the Federal Reserve System and the *Federal Reserve Bulletin*.

APPENDIX C

REGRESSION EQUATIONS FOR ESTIMATING MONTHLY AVERAGE DAILY FREE-RESERVE RATIOS

(Parentheses under the coefficients contain the standard errors of the coefficients. Brackets contain coefficients of partial determination, the coefficients of partial correlation squared.)

Equation Number	Period	Regression Equation	Coefficient of Multiple Determination, R^2
T13	Jan., 1947—Dec., 1958	$100 (R_F/D) = \underset{(0.0200)}{0.835} + \underset{\substack{(0.0939)\\ [0.00774]}}{0.0985\, r_d} - \underset{\substack{(0.0711)\\ [0.232]}}{0.464\, r_b}$	0.627
T14	Jan., 1947—Dec., 1958	$100 (R_F/D) = 0.839 + \underset{[0.00730]}{0.0955\, r_d} - \underset{[0.232]}{0.463\, r_b} + \underset{[0.00450]}{9.01\, d(R_F/D)/dt}$	0.629
T15	Jan., 1947—Dec., 1958	$100 (R_F/D) = 0.836 + \underset{[0.00616]}{0.0874\, r_d} - \underset{[0.228]}{0.457\, r_b} - \underset{[0.00213]}{11.0\, d(R_F/D)/dt} + \underset{[0.0101]}{0.0278\, \phi}$	0.633
T16	July, 1951—Dec., 1958	$100 (R_F/D) = 0.394 + \underset{[0.0618]}{0.242\, r_d} - \underset{[0.297]}{0.444\, r_b} - \underset{[0.00343]}{12.2\, d(R_F/D)/dt} + \underset{[0.0194]}{0.0343\, \phi}$	0.503
T17	July, 1951—Dec., 1958	$100 (R_F/D) = 0.997 - \underset{[0.453]}{1.090\, r_b/r_d} + \underset{[0.0954]}{0.051\, \phi}$	0.503
T18	Jan., 1947—Dec., 1958	$100 (R_F/D) = \underset{(0.0201)}{1.168} - \underset{\substack{(0.0821)\\ [0.0000605]}}{0.00756\, r_d} - \underset{\substack{(0.0651)\\ [0.220]}}{0.409\, r_{3-5}} + \underset{\substack{(0.0131)\\ [0.0124]}}{0.0173\, \phi}$	0.627
T19	Jan., 1947—Dec., 1958	$100 (R_F/D) = \underset{(0.0192)}{0.949} - \underset{\substack{(0.764)\\ [0.0860]}}{0.277\, (r_b - r_d)} - \underset{\substack{(0.0322)\\ [0.451]}}{0.345\, r_{3-5}} + \underset{\substack{(0.0125)\\ [0.0101]}}{0.0149\, \phi}$	0.659
T20	Jan., 1947—Dec., 1958	$100 (R_F/D) = \underset{(0.0188)}{1.442} - \underset{\substack{(0.132)\\ [0.128]}}{0.597\, r_b/r_d} - \underset{\substack{(0.0340)\\ [0.374]}}{0.311\, r_{3-5}} + \underset{\substack{(0.0122)\\ [0.0121]}}{0.0159\, \phi}$	0.675

APPENDIX C—*Continued*

Equation Number	Period	Regression Equation	Coefficient of Multiple Determination, R^2
T21	Feb., 1947— Dec., 1958	$100\,(R_P/D)_t =$ 1.417 (0.0181) $-0.556\,(r_b/r_a)_t$ (0.130) [0.116] $-0.318\,(r_{3-5})_t$ (0.0329) [0.402] $+\,0.0430\,\phi_{t-1}$ (0.0181) [0.0868]	0.697
T22	Feb., 1947— Dec., 1958	$100\,(R_P/D)_t =$ 1.409 (0.0180) $-0.549\,(r_b/r_a)_t$ (0.129) [0.115] $-0.321\,(r_{3-5})_t$ (0.0327) [0.410] $+\,0.0726\,(\phi_t+\phi_{t-1})/2$ (0.0185) [0.100]	0.701
T23	Jan., 1954— Dec., 1959	$100\,(R_P/D) =$ 0.561 (0.0183) $+0.00687\,r_d$ (0.0742) [0.000126] $-0.251\,r_b$ (0.0540) [0.241] $+\,0.0155\,\phi$ (0.0151) [0.0152]	0.726
T24	Jan., 1954— Dec., 1959	$100\,(R_P/D)_t =$ 0.500 $+0.0338\,(r_a)_{t-1}$ (0.0734) [0.00312] $-0.262\,(r_b)_{t-1}$ (0.0540) [0.258] $+\,0.0606\,\phi_{t-1}$ (0.0144) [0.207]	0.731
T25	Jan., 1954— Dec., 1959	$100\,(R_P/D)_t =$ 0.921 (0.0195) $-0.463\,(r_b/r_a)_t$ (0.147) [0.127] $+0.0313\,\phi_{t-1}$ (0.0160) [0.0535] $-\,0.168\,(r_{3-5})_t$ (0.0341) [0.263]	0.688
T26	Jan., 1954— Dec., 1959	$100\,(R_P/D)_t =$ 0.927 (0.0192) $-0.491\,(r_b/r_a)_{t-1}$ (0.141) [0.152] $-0.165\,r_{3-5}$ (0.0341) [0.257] $+\,0.0479\,\phi_{t-1}$ (0.0151) [0.128]	0.698
T27	Feb., 1954— Dec., 1959	$100\,(R_P/D)_t =$ 0.868 (0.0184) $-0.440\,(r_b/r_a)_{t-1}$ (0.140) [0.129] $-0.164\,(r_{3-5})_{t-1}$ (0.0330) [0.269] $+\,0.0671\,(\phi_{t-1}+\phi_{t-2})/2$ (0.0217) [0.125]	0.709
T28	Jan., 1954— Dec., 1959	$100\,(R_P/D) =$ 0.970 (0.0193) $-0.553\,r_b/r_d$ (0.154) [0.159] $-0.159\,r_{3-5}$ (0.0353) [0.231] $+\,0.0401\,\phi$ (0.0224) [0.0449]	0.694

100

Equation Number	Period	Regression Equation	Coefficient of Multiple Determination, R^2
T29	Jan., 1954—Dec., 1959	$100\,(R_F/D)_t = 0.532\ (0.0171)\ -0.232\,(r_b)_t\ (0.0185)\ [0.700]\ +0.0394\,\phi_{t-1}\ (0.0141)\ [0.103]\ -0.115\,\Delta r_d\ (0.127)\ [0.0118]$	0.760
T30	Jan., 1954—Dec., 1959	$100\,(R_F/D)_t = 0.544\ (0.0171)\ +0.0392\,\Delta r_b\ (0.0730)\ [0.00422]\ -0.240\,(r_b)_t\ (0.0179)\ [0.725]\ +0.0460\,\phi_{t-1}\ (0.0145)\ [0.128]$	0.758
T31	Jan., 1954—Dec., 1959	$100\,(R_F/D)_t = -0.439\ (0.0156)\ +0.778\,(1/r_b)_t\ (0.0504)\ [0.776]\ +0.0319\,\phi_{t-1}\ (0.0124)\ [0.0876]$	0.798
T32	Jan., 1954—Dec., 1959	$100\,(R_F/D)_t = -0.0604\ (0.0148)\ -0.107\,(r_d)_t\ (0.0362)\ [0.114]\ +0.571\,(1/r_b)_t\ (0.0849)\ [0.400]\ +0.0394\,\phi_{t-1}\ (0.0120)\ [0.136]$	0.821
T33	Jan., 1954—Dec., 1959	$100\,(R_F/D)_t = -0.609\ (0.0146)\ +0.741\,(1/r_d)_t\ (0.232)\ [0.130]\ +0.491\,(1/r_b)_t\ (0.102)\ [0.256]\ +0.0431\,\phi_{t-1}\ (0.0122)\ [0.156]$	0.824
T34	Feb., 1954—Dec., 1959	$100\,(R_F/D)_t = -0.636\ (0.0137)\ +0.989\,(1/r_d)_t\ (0.215)\ [0.207]\ +0.394\,(1/r_b)_t\ (0.0961)\ [0.200]\ +0.0696\,(\phi_{t-1}+\phi_{t-2})/2\ (0.0164)\ [0.211]$	0.851
T35	Feb., 1954—Dec., 1959	$100\,(R_F/D)_t = 0.508\ (0.0163)\ -0.228\ (0.0168)\ [0.730]\ +0.675\,(\phi_{t-1}+\phi_{t-2})/2\ (0.0185)\ [0.164]$	0.770
T36	Jan., 1954—Dec., 1959	$100\,(R_F/D)_t = -0.251\,(r_b)_t +0.047\,\phi_{t-1} +0.606\,S_1 +0.628\,S_2 +0.558\,S_3$ $+0.518\,S_4 +0.476\,S_5 +0.534\,S_6 +0.503\,S_7 +0.540\,S_8$ $+0.630\,S_9 +0.611\,S_{10} +0.579\,S_{11} +0.676\,S_{12}$	0.91

Free Reserves and the Money Supply

In fitting some of the early regression equations of the study, the computer was not programed to produce the standard errors of the regression coefficients. The coefficients of partial correlation were used for tests of significance. For later work the program was improved in order to produce the standard errors of the coefficients. The subscript t in the equations containing lagged variables refers to a time interval of one month. A subscript $t - 1$ identifies the month prior to month t. In the equations without t subscripts all variables pertain to the same time periods.

D = total monthly daily-average member bank deposits subject to reserve requirements.

R_F = monthly daily-average free reserves.

$\phi = [1/R_U][dR_U/dt] - [D/R_U][d(R_R/D)/dt]$ = monthly per cent change in unborrowed reserves adjusted for reserve requirement changes.

r_b = Treasury bill rate.

r_d = New York discount rate.

r_{3-5} = monthly daily-average market yield on 3–5-year Treasury securities.

S = a proxy seasonal variable assumed to be equal to zero except in the month indicated by its subscript number. The subscript numbers run from 1 through 12 for the 12 calendar months.

Sources: J.1 Releases of the Board of Governors of the Federal Reserve System and the *Federal Reserve Bulletin*.

APPENDIX D

DATA EMPLOYED IN THE REGRESSION EQUATIONS

Year and Month	D	R	R_R	R_B	$100\,(R_F/D)$	$(1/D)(dD/dt)$	$(1/R_U)(dR_U/dt)$	ϕ
1947 1	103938.	16401.	15549.	105.	0.717735	−0.953935	−1.911572	−1.572027
2	102141.	15996.	15196.	203.	.584483	−1.337361	−1.700121	−1.182190
3	101916.	16008.	15134.	171.	.689289	−0.160426	−0.337817	−0.247809
4	101761.	15930.	15097.	126.	.694270	0.560133	0.572640	0.472307
5	102329.	15977.	15193.	106.	.661588	0.485197	0.482026	0.480403
6	103362.	16153.	15368.	135.	.628858	1.135814	1.476418	1.304821
7	104511.	16346.	15563.	92.	.660692	0.947743	0.953612	0.818002
8	105221.	16481.	15680.	127.	.640556	0.961310	1.381925	1.286027
9	106711.	16865.	15934.	133.	.747814	1.287121	1.706260	1.533019
10	107820.	17071.	16118.	170.	.726674	0.639955	−0.044376	−0.061501
11	107971.	16986.	16136.	274.	.532547	0.189864	−0.421866	−0.534518
12	108610.	17254.	16272.	225.	.696529	0.714482	3.579188	3.430545
1948 1	108920.	17395.	16309.	142.	.866691	−0.613753	−2.854576	−2.578686
2	107266.	16832.	16028.	244.	.521598	−1.297703	−0.174826	−1.526812
3	106435.	17112.	16288.	266.	.523793	−1.165501	−0.887478	−1.607773
4	105576.	16925.	16115.	111.	.661605	0.215483	1.079457	0.985928
5	105951.	16935.	16190.	143.	.568656	0.196788	0.407920	−0.030046
6	106208.	17395.	16544.	100.	.707570	−0.068262	2.633633	0.373911
7	106299.	17531.	16706.	95.	.686738	0.783164	1.066758	1.105823
8	107039.	17691.	16825.	87.	.728239	0.442362	0.900337	0.658944
9	107683.	18509.	17625.	128.	.702060	0.387712	8.288224	−0.730887
10	107887.	19817.	19001.	112.	.652535	0.313291	2.560199	0.771703
11	108173.	19834.	19064.	118.	.602735	0.197830	−0.192738	−0.346246
12	108632.	19986.	19190.	133.	.609854	0.515499	1.201329	1.135030
1949 1	108629.	19996.	19154.	168.	.619997	−0.723101	−1.853487	−1.578170
2	107330.	19565.	18855.	109.	.559489	−0.898165	−0.832670	−0.537668
3	106816.	19421.	18726.	146.	0.513965	−0.977378	−1.517511	−1.171370

APPENDIX D—*Continued*

Year and Month	D	R	R_R	R_B	$100\ (R_F/D)$	$(1/D)(dD/dt)$	$(1/R_U)(dR_U/dt)$	ϕ
1949 4	105715.	19185.	18479.	98.	0.575131	−0.439389	−2.920837	−0.428056
5	105381.	18153.	17373.	176.	.572681	−0.115770	−3.593581	0.270398
6	105673.	18068.	17310.	100.	.622672	0.218597	−0.712379	1.503932
7	105764.	17566.	16538.	106.	.870802	0.580062	−3.556804	−0.404871
8	107121.	16885.	15932.	93.	.802364	1.300398	−5.639591	2.457800
9	108161.	16083.	15161.	75.	.783088	0.699416	−1.383683	−0.041047
10	108817.	16114.	15249.	45.	.753558	0.571601	−0.015558	0.010396
11	109213.	16119.	15308.	134.	.620347	0.451869	−0.175160	−0.386190
12	110116.	16288.	15486.	120.	.619347	0.954448	3.247054	3.099903
1950 1	110890.	16527.	15585.	34.	.818375	−0.085671	−2.237381	−1.962817
2	110125.	16143.	15407.	119.	.559818	−0.625653	−0.396281	−0.021687
3	109654.	16085.	15298.	126.	.602348	−0.394879	−1.726354	−1.449966
4	109243.	15898.	15204.	101.	.542366	−0.135478	0.237394	0.347424
5	109489.	15942.	15235.	79.	.572658	0.651660	0.639874	0.519207
6	110550.	16193.	15426.	68.	.632745	0.862505	1.776689	1.546995
7	111055.	16255.	15506.	121.	.565482	0.240420	−1.289164	−1.340010
8	111642.	16272.	15623.	160.	.437557	1.005441	1.896102	1.524948
9	112753.	16602.	15837.	96.	.593330	0.424820	1.338906	1.234034
10	113127.	16728.	15886.	66.	.685509	0.708934	0.909282	0.853142
11	113914.	16742.	16009.	145.	.516176	0.848443	0.970025	0.660225
12	115716.	17387.	16360.	141.	.765664	1.610401	3.435578	2.451008
1951 1	116344.	18075.	17244.	209.	.534191	−0.471877	4.866786	−3.742996
2	115602.	18909.	18280.	326.	.261672	−0.022924	2.612602	0.966252
3	116519.	19205.	18491.	240.	.406800	0.742368	1.618771	1.257746
4	116490.	19323.	18491.	161.	.576444	−0.455834	−1.795174	−1.569456
5	115740.	18894.	18303.	440.	.130465	−0.325730	0.124634	0.364249
6	116567.	19308.	18475.	170.	.568772	0.997709	1.604097	1.345761
7	116825.	19230.	18473.	193.	.481915	−0.098010	−0.743309	−0.350264
8	117054.	19175.	18469.	292.	0.353255	0.357527	−0.672564	−0.582291

APPENDIX D—*Continued*

Year and Month		D	R	R_R	R_B	$100\,(R_F/D)$	$(1/D)(dD/dt)$	$(1/R_U)(dR_U/dt)$	ϕ
1951	9	118176.	19396.	18675.	337.	0.324091	1.538799	3.738489	3.417618
	10	119727.	19865.	18949.	95.	.685726	0.960936	0.187147	0.260603
	11	120596.	19793.	19064.	340.	.322564	0.831288	-1.094919	-1.207183
	12	122629.	20297.	19476.	658.	.132921	1.796883	4.025051	3.645091
1952	1	123177.	20470.	19537.	210.	.586957	-0.565445	-0.863772	-0.503217
	2	122137.	19992.	19297.	366.	.268960	-0.861328	-2.675023	-2.317491
	3	122291.	20195.	19318.	311.	.463239	0.464465	2.579899	2.537711
	4	121548.	19777.	19127.	367.	.232828	-0.652415	-3.933540	-3.589018
	5	121676.	19767.	19138.	563.	.053831	0.532560	-0.210899	-0.219087
	6	123260.	20140.	19251.	579.	.251094	2.420889	3.435407	3.709280
	7	125842.	20538.	19928.	1073.	-.368318	0.153763	-2.784557	-3.432810
	8	124836.	20307.	19655.	1032.	-.304799	-0.467813	-0.184177	0.266577
	9	125490.	20514.	19735.	683.	-.075703	1.184955	3.320642	3.221433
	10	126908.	20607.	19959.	1047.	-.314401	0.856917	-2.926892	-2.791353
	11	127824.	20744.	20087.	1532.	-.684924	1.248587	-0.106705	-0.376342
	12	129713.	21173.	20454.	1595.	-.675720	0.759365	2.181019	2.240508
1953	1	129092.	20963.	20253.	1351.	-.496546	-1.380411	-2.197579	-1.527280
	2	127403.	20514.	19879.	1295.	-.518040	-0.706810	-0.621765	-0.261411
	3	127195.	20414.	19827.	1206.	-.486260	-0.555445	-0.593488	-0.371646
	4	125592.	20007.	19472.	1166.	-.502817	-1.021957	-1.642695	-1.172237
	5	124862.	19897.	19306.	952.	-.289920	-0.101712	3.204096	3.340236
	6	125891.	20287.	19499.	423.	-.289535	0.637056	1.726742	3.433474
	7	127677.	19651.	18861.	415.	.293710	2.972736	-3.774076	-0.190588
	8	129173.	19528.	18884.	653.	-.006968	-0.571325	-0.757616	-0.357647
	9	129116.	19552.	18834.	468.	.192848	0.115399	1.729242	1.890392
	10	129132.	19534.	18783.	365.	.299306	0.524269	0.320822	0.526623
	11	130716.	19718.	19034.	487.	.150707	1.178122	-0.174194	-0.433407
	12	131869.	19914.	19224.	444.	0.186169	0.827715	3.377076	3.439105

105

APPENDIX D—*Continued*

Year and Month		D	R	R_R	R_B	$100\,(R_F/D)$	$(1/D)(dD/dt)$	$(1/R_U)(dR_U/dt)$	ϕ
1954	1	132254.	20177.	19244.	101.	0.629089	−0.652152	−0.941424	−0.581637
	2	130724.	19555.	18921.	289.	.263914	−0.822726	−2.151404	−1.707292
	3	130730.	19569.	18880.	339.	.267727	−0.188174	−0.572024	−0.295563
	4	129589.	19390.	18627.	139.	.481522	−0.190217	0.883071	1.064261
	5	130706.	19529.	18814.	155.	.428823	1.134985	1.205192	1.078710
	6	132015.	19670.	18813.	146.	.538572	0.730596	1.423889	1.289585
	7	132475.	19167.	18331.	65.	.581996	0.536704	−2.973511	0.592466
	8	133796.	18480.	17639.	115.	.542991	0.468997	−2.368572	−0.004100
	9	134028.	18403.	17628.	67.	.528245	1.381795	1.559773	1.342725
	10	137354.	18891.	18171.	82.	.464493	1.757866	2.195757	1.888772
	11	138789.	19206.	18392.	170.	.464013	0.938835	−0.267907	−0.603247
	12	139781.	19276.	18573.	246.	.326582	0.384529	0.420400	0.485373
1955	1	139274.	19116.	18432.	313.	.266021	−0.791244	−2.005000	−1.587185
	2	137947.	18811.	18188.	353.	.195364	−1.007997	−1.752628	−1.405669
	3	137172.	18634.	18050.	460.	.090397	0.067433	−0.784087	−0.796828
	4	138070.	18800.	18210.	494.	.069530	0.491777	1.423030	1.291521
	5	137943.	18748.	18166.	366.	.156586	−0.287439	−1.191351	−0.898704
	6	138056.	18715.	18166.	401.	.106840	0.286477	0.401343	0.352204
	7	138472.	18822.	18201.	529.	−.065717	0.509487	−0.363538	−0.334661
	8	138351.	18731.	18152.	768.	−.136610	−0.403684	−1.731289	−1.399567
	9	138547.	18711.	18148.	848.	−.205706	0.492610	−0.251918	−0.193587
	10	139835.	18868.	18342.	886.	−.257445	0.866017	0.283616	0.151186
	11	140150.	18902.	18378.	1016.	−.351053	0.161255	0.668120	0.521026
	12	141517.	19230.	18639.	840.	−.176657	1.406539	3.501998	3.104485
1956	1	141364.	19144.	18590.	804.	−.177202	−1.839571	−3.961288	−3.343245
	2	138974.	18708.	18176.	795.	−.188885	−0.643646	−0.192593	0.029515
	3	139852.	18918.	18335.	989.	−.290307	0.979607	−0.108763	−0.394248
	4	139940.	18847.	18320.	1060.	−0.380879	−0.232600	−0.922022	−0.712251

APPENDIX D—*Continued*

Year and Month	D	R	R_R	R_B	100 (R_F/D)	$(1/D)(dD/dt)$	$(1\ R_U)(dR_U/dt)$	ϕ
1956 5	139741.	18736.	18268.	975.	−0.363530	−0.150278	1.131724	1.351414
6	140470.	18933.	18359.	768.	−.138464	0.731829	1.500178	1.465855
7	140016.	18840.	18239.	741.	−.100346	−1.109156	−1.859220	−1.361206
8	139929.	18777.	18217.	898.	−.242266	1.379271	1.266885	0.950206
9	141545.	19024.	18445.	792.	−.150482	0.253628	0.633484	0.840944
10	141643.	18938.	18416.	718.	−.138729	0.306402	0.181119	0.249461
11	142561.	19169.	18579.	743.	−.107674	0.897156	2.255027	1.767874
12	144181.	19523.	18877.	685.	−.026703	1.323683	2.226822	2.086499
1957 1	144177.	19301.	18777.	405.	−.081843	−1.727038	−3.320897	−2.370463
2	141648.	18813.	18299.	639.	−.088953	−0.812578	−2.217515	−1.739245
3	142272.	18880.	18361.	833.	−.221055	1.311216	−0.257661	−0.331099
4	143967.	19086.	18580.	1010.	−.350081	0.335840	0.652799	0.801847
5	142988.	18830.	18365.	911.	−.311914	−0.622428	−1.308667	−0.771208
6	143895.	18981.	18485.	1004.	−.353382	1.273493	0.834399	0.516398
7	144791.	19132.	18597.	926.	−.269699	−0.685124	0.151045	0.651064
8	143243.	18834.	18298.	1008.	−.329860	−0.119727	−0.833077	−0.594992
9	144318.	18955.	18433.	988.	−.322897	1.184532	0.862692	0.781493
10	145507.	19042.	18575.	816.	−.240539	−0.227481	0.713286	1.017223
11	144712.	18958.	18447.	804.	−.202127	0.210763	0.630697	0.350158
12	147019.	19409.	18837.	709.	−.093185	1.848734	3.288682	3.059188
1958 1	147026.	19302.	18728.	456.	.079578	−1.285143	−0.859622	0.192282
2	146127.	19004.	18430.	238.	.229593	0.480060	−0.402324	1.490468
3	148270.	18727.	18096.	137.	.332838	1.335064	−1.627263	1.680072
4	150169.	18395.	17771.	129.	.328629	1.884537	−0.886943	1.759048
5	151326.	18224.	17558.	119.	.360808	0.175118	−0.665599	0.104720
6	154302.	18600.	17974.	142.	.313669	2.419922	3.058294	2.613284
7	154798.	18611.	17955.	110.	.352393	−0.647617	−1.302632	−0.671300
8	155065.	18581.	17945.	250.	0.248926	0.348562	−1.852055	−1.639013

APPENDIX D—*Continued*

Year and Month		D	R	R_R	R_B	$100\ (R_R/D)$	$(1/D)(dD/dt)$	$(1/R_V)(dR_V/dt)$	ϕ
1958	9	154860.	18425.	17854.	476.	0.061022	−0.212450	−0.802296	−0.543235
	10	155664.	18473.	17952.	425.	.061350	0.693802	0.590109	0.520668
	11	156194.	18541.	18034.	485.	.013125	0.740105	0.670174	0.269765
	12	158381.	18891.	18377.	553.	.025256	1.460713	1.251534	1.042028
1959	1	159068.	18896.	18397.	560.	−.038349	−0.665752	−0.894416	−0.381338
	2	157248.	18568.	18109.	504.	−.029254	−1.272195	−2.048330	−1.610657
	3	156389.	18426.	17966.	600.	−.089841	0.813356	0.406709	0.293583
	4	158561.	18664.	18246.	676.	−.162714	0.539225	−0.072269	0.054935
	5	158065.	18582.	18133.	766.	−.200550	−0.636762	−1.998204	−1.604611
	6	157641.	18451.	18043.	921.	−.325741	0.512240	0.042784	−0.057067
	7	159106.	18665.	18266.	957.	−.351339	0.551205	0.906395	0.632196
	8	158298.	18614.	18141.	1009.	−.338286	−0.578972	−0.897448	−0.637535
	9	158612.	18593.	18183.	902.	−.310507	0.165498	0.599191	0.571324
	10	158427.	18609.	18161.	908.	−.290670	0.222499	0.833309	0.649584
	11	158295.	18621.	18176.	878.	−.273541	−0.313339	−0.360706	−0.574485
	12	159760.	18955.	18444.	921.	−0.256322	1.429640	2.098755	1.620341

[Notes to Appendix D are on page 109.]

All items have been computed from semimonthly daily-average data and are centered on midmonths. The deposit estimate recorded for a particular month, therefore, is the mean of the daily average deposits in the two semimonthly periods of that month.

D = daily-average member-bank net demand deposits subject to reserve requirements plus daily-average member-bank time deposits. Net demand deposits subject to reserve requirements are total demand deposits minus cash items in process of collection minus demand balances due from domestic banks (also minus war loan and Series E bond accounts until June 30, 1947), in millions of dollars.

R = total daily-average member-bank reserve balances at Federal Reserve Banks (and a portion of vault cash allowable as reserves beginning in December, 1959), in millions of dollars.

R_R = total daily-average required reserves, in millions of dollars.

R_B = total daily-average member bank borrowings at Federal Reserve Banks, in millions of dollars.

R_F/D = ratio of total daily-average free reserves (excess reserves minus borrowings) to total deposits subject to reserve requirements.

$(1/D)(dD/dt)$ = rate of change of total deposits in per cent per month (decimal point has been shifted to express in per cent per month), at midmonth.

$(1/R_U)(dR_U/dt)$ = rate of change of unborrowed reserves (total reserves minus borrowings) in per cent per month, at midmonth.

ϕ = rate of change of unborrowed reserves adjusted for reserve requirement-changes, in per cent per month, at midmonth.

Source: J.1 Releases of the Board of Governors of the Federal Reserve System, "Deposits, Reserves, and Borrowings of Member Banks."

109

Bibliography

BLACK, ROBERT P. "An Analysis of the Impacts of the 1953 and 1954 Reductions in Federal Reserve Member Bank Reserve Requirements." Unpublished Ph.D. dissertation, Graduate Faculty of the University of Virginia, 1955.

BOARD OF GOVERNORS OF THE FEDERAL RESERVE SYSTEM [formerly Federal Reserve Board]. *Tenth Annual Report of the Federal Reserve Board Covering Operations for the Year 1923.* Washington: Government Printing Office, 1924.

―――. *Eleventh Annual Report of the Federal Reserve Board Covering Operations for the Year 1924.* Washington: Government Printing Office, 1925.

―――. *Twelfth Annual Report of the Federal Reserve Board Covering Operations for the Year 1925.* Washington: Government Printing Office, 1926.

―――. *Thirteenth Annual Report of the Federal Reserve Board Covering Operations for the Year 1926.* Washington: Government Printing Office, 1927.

―――. *Fifteenth Annual Report of the Federal Reserve Board Covering Operations for the Year 1928.* Washington: Government Printing Office, 1929.

―――. *Twenty-fourth Annual Report of the Board of Governors of the Federal Reserve System Covering Operations for the Year 1937.* Washington: Board of Governors of the Federal Reserve System, 1938.

―――. *Twenty-fifth Annual Report of the Board of Governors of the Federal Reserve System Covering Operations for the Year 1938.* Washington: Board of Governors of the Federal Reserve System, 1939.

―――. *Twenty-sixth Annual Report of the Board of Governors of the Federal Reserve System Covering Operations for the Year 1939.* Washington: Board of Governors of the Federal Reserve System, 1940.

―――. *Forty-fourth Annual Report of the Board of Governors of the Federal Reserve System Covering Operations for the Year 1957.* Washington: Board of Governors of the Federal Reserve System, 1958.

―――. *Banking and Monetary Statistics.* Washington: Board of Governors of the Federal Reserve System, 1943.

―――. "Excess Profits Taxes of Commercial Banks," *Federal Reserve Bulletin,* XXXVII (June, 1952), 602–19.

―――. *The Federal Funds Market—A Study by a Federal Reserve System Committee.* Washington: Board of Governors of the Federal Reserve System, 1957.

―――. *The Federal Reserve System: Purposes and Functions.* 4th ed. Washington: Board of Governors of the Federal Reserve System, 1961.

BRUNNER, KARL. "Some Major Problems in Monetary Theory," *American Economic Review,* LI, No. 2 (May, 1961), 47–56.

112   *Free Reserves and the Money Supply*

BRYAN, WILLIAM R. "Bank Purchases of Earning Assets: A Decision Unit Model." Unpublished Ph.D. dissertation, University of Wisconsin, 1961.

BURGESS, W. RANDOLPH. *The Reserve Banks and the Money Market*. Rev. ed. New York: Harper & Bros., 1936.

———. "Factors Affecting Changes in Short Term Interest Rates," *Journal of the American Statistical Association*, XXII, New Series, No. 158 (June, 1927), 195–201.

CAMPBELL, COLIN D. *The Federal Reserve and the Business Cycle*. (Tuck Bulletin 26.) Hanover, New Hampshire: Amos Tuck School of Business Administration, 1961.

CARR, HOBART C. "Why and How To Read the Federal Reserve Statement," *Journal of Finance*, XIV (December, 1959), 504–19.

CHANDLER, LESTER. *Benjamin Strong, Central Banker*. Washington: Brookings Institution, 1958.

CRICK, W. F. "The Genesis of Bank Deposits," *Economica*, VII (1927), 191–202. Reprinted in *Readings in Monetary Theory*. Ed. by FRIEDRICH A. LUTZ and LLOYD W. MINTS. New York: Blakiston Co., 1951. Pp. 41–53.

CULBERTSON, JOHN M. "Timing Changes in Monetary Policy," *Journal of Finance*, XIV (May, 1959), 145–60.

CURRIE, LAUCHLIN. *The Supply and Control of Money in the United States*. 2d ed., rev. Cambridge, Mass.: Harvard University Press, 1935.

EZEKIEL, MORDECAI, and FOX, KARL A. *Methods of Correlation and Regression Analysis, Linear and Curvilinear*. 3d ed. New York: John Wiley & Sons, 1959.

FEDERAL RESERVE BANK OF NEW YORK. *Bank Reserves: Some Major Factors Affecting Them*. 2d ed. New York: Federal Reserve Bank of New York, 1954.

———. "Borrowing from the Fed," *Monthly Review*, September, 1959, pp. 138–42.

———. *Money Market Essays*. New York: Federal Reserve Bank of New York, 1952.

———. "The Significance and Limitations of Free Reserves," *Monthly Review*, November, 1958, pp. 162–67.

———. *The Treasury and the Money Market*. New York: Federal Reserve Bank of New York, 1954.

FEDERAL RESERVE BANK OF PHILADELPHIA. "Discount Rate and the Discount Policy," *Business Review*, January, 1959, pp. 12–26.

FEDERAL RESERVE BANK OF ST. LOUIS. "A New Measure of the Money Supply," *Monthly Review*, July, 1959, pp. 77–83.

———. "Vault Cash as Bank Reserves," *Monthly Review*, December, 1959, pp. 134–35.

FINNEY, KATHERINE. *Interbank Deposits: The Purpose and Effects of Domestic Balances, 1934–54*. New York: Columbia University Press, 1958.

FISHER, IRVING. *The Theory of Interest*. New York: Kelley & Millman, Inc., 1954.

FREUTEL, GUY S. "Income and Product Analysis for an Open Regional Economy: The Eighth Federal Reserve District." Unpublished Ph.D. dissertation, Department of Economics, Harvard University, 1956.

FRIEDMAN, MILTON. "Notes on Lectures in Price Theory." Notes on Lectures given January–June, 1951, in Economics 300*A* and 300*B*, University of Chicago.

———. *A Program for Monetary Stability.* (The Millar Lectures, No. 3, 1959.) New York: Fordham University Press, 1960.

GOLDENWEISER, E. A. *American Monetary Policy.* 1st ed. New York: McGraw-Hill Book Co., 1951.

HARDY, CHARLES O. *Credit Policies of the Federal Reserve System.* Washington: Brookings Institution, 1932.

HARRIS, SEYMOUR E. *Twenty Years of Federal Reserve Policy.* 2 vols. Cambridge, Mass.: Harvard University Press, 1933.

HART, ALBERT G. *Money, Debt, and Economic Activity.* 2d ed. New York: Prentice-Hall, Inc., 1953.

HAYWOOD, CHARLES F. "The Adequacy of Federal Reserve Powers To Discharge Responsibilities," *Journal of Finance,* XIV, No. 2 (May, 1959), 135–44.

HORWICH, GEORGE. "Elements of Timing and Response in the Balance Sheet of Banking, 1953–55," *Journal of Finance,* XII (May, 1957), 238–55.

KAREKEN, JOHN H. "Our Knowledge of Monetary Policy," *American Economic Review,* LI, No. 2 (May, 1961), 41–44.

KEYNES, JOHN MAYNARD. *A Tract on Monetary Reform.* London: Macmillan Co., 1923.

———. *A Treatise on Money.* 2 vols. New York: Harcourt, Brace & Co., 1930.

KLEIN, L. R. *A Textbook of Econometrics.* Evanston Ill.: Row, Peterson & Co., 1956.

KLEIN, L. R., and GOLDBERGER, A. S. *An Econometric Model of the United States, 1929–1952.* Amsterdam: North-Holland Publishing Co., 1955.

McDONALD, STEPHEN L. "The Internal Drain and Bank Credit Expansion," *Journal of Finance,* VIII (December, 1953), 407–21.

McKINNEY, GEORGE W., JR. *The Federal Reserve Discount Window.* New Brunswick, N.J.: Rutgers University Press, 1960.

MELTZER, ALLAN H. "The Behavior of the French Money Supply: 1938–54," *Journal of Political Economy,* LXVII (June, 1959), 275–96.

MINTS, LLOYD W. *A History of Banking Theory in Great Britain and the United States.* Chicago: University of Chicago Press, 1945.

———. *Monetary Policy for a Competitive Society.* New York: McGraw-Hill Book Co., 1950.

MORRISON, GEORGE R. "Portfolio Behavior of Banks." Ph.D. dissertation, University of Chicago. In process.

PHILLIPS, CHESTER ARTHUR. *Bank Credit.* New York: Macmillan Co., 1921.

POLAK, J. J., and WHITE, WILLIAM H. "The Effect of Income Expansion on the Quantity of Money," *International Monetary Fund: Staff Papers*, IV (August, 1955), 398–433.

POLAKOFF, MURRAY E. "Reluctance Elasticity, Least Cost, and Member-Bank Borrowing: A Suggested Integration," *Journal of Finance*, XV (March, 1960), 1–18.

RIEFLER, WINFIELD W. *Money Rates and Money Markets in the United States.* New York: Harper & Bros., 1930.

———. "Open Market Operations in Long-Term Securities," *Federal Reserve Bulletin*, XLIV, No. 11 (November, 1958), 1260–74.

ROOSA, ROBERT V. "Credit Policy at the Discount Window: Comment," *Quarterly Journal of Economics*, LXXIII, No. 2 (May, 1959), 333–37.

———. *Federal Reserve Operations in the Money and Government Securities Markets.* New York: Federal Reserve Bank of New York, 1956.

———. "Monetary and Credit Policy," in *Economics and the Policy Maker.* (Brookings Lectures, 1958–59.) Washington: Brookings Institution, 1959. Pp. 89–116.

SCOTT, IRA. "The Changing Significance of Treasury Obligations in Commercial Bank Portfolios," *Journal of Finance*, XII (May, 1957), 213–22.

SIMMONS, EDWARD C. "Federal Reserve Discount Rate Policy and Member Bank Borrowing, 1944–50," *Journal of Business of the University of Chicago*, XXV, No. 1 (January, 1952), 18–29.

———. "The Monetary Mechanism since the War," *Journal of Political Economy*, LVII (April, 1950), 124–41.

———. "A Note on the Causes of Instability in the Money Supply," *Journal of Finance*, VI (September, 1951), 333–37.

———. "A Note on the Revival of Federal Reserve Discount Policy," *Journal of Finance*, XI (December, 1956), 413–21.

SMITH, WARREN L. "The Discount Rate as a Credit-Control Weapon," *Journal of Political Economy*, XLVI (April, 1958), 171–77.

SPRINKEL, BERYL W. "Monetary Growth as a Cyclical Predictor," *Journal of Finance*, XIV (September, 1959), 333–46.

TINBERGEN, JAN. *Business Cycles in the United States of America, 1919–1937.* Geneva: League of Nations, 1939.

———. *Econometrics.* New York: Blakiston Co., 1951.

TOLLEY, GEORGE S. "Providing for Growth of the Money Supply," *Journal of Political Economy*, LXV (December, 1957), 465–85.

TURNER, ROBERT C. *Member-Bank Borrowing.* Columbus: Ohio State University, 1938.

U.S. ANNUAL REPORT of the Secretary of the Treasury on the State of the Finances, for the Fiscal Year Ended June 30, 1951, Treasury Document No. 3177. Washington: United States Government Printing Office, 1952.

U.S. 1939 INTERNAL REVENUE CODE. Excess Profits Taxes, Secs. 430, 431, 434, 436, and 437.

WALKER, CHARLS E. "Discount Policy in the Light of Recent Experience," *Journal of Finance*, XII (May, 1957), 223–37.

WARBURTON, CLARK. "Bank Reserves and Business Fluctuations," *Journal of the American Statistical Association*, XLIII (December, 1948), 547–58.

————. "Monetary Control under the Federal Reserve Act," *Political Science Quarterly*, LXI (December, 1946), 505–34.

————. "Monetary Velocity and Monetary Policy," *Review of Economics and Statistics*, XXX (November, 1948), 304–14.

WHITTLESEY, CHARLES R. "Credit Policy at the Discount Window," *Quarterly Journal of Economics*, LXXIII (May, 1959), 207–16.

YOUNG, RALPH A. "Tools and Processes of Monetary Policy," in *United States Monetary Policy*. New York: American Assembly, Columbia University, December, 1958. Pp. 13–48.

Index

Black, Robert P., 25, 26, 82
Bond-support policy, influence on free-reserve ratio, 71, 72
Borrowing by member banks
  determinants of, 7–9, 10, 15, 19–21, 88–90
  influence on deposit expansion, 10–14
  influence on interest rates, 8–10, 12, 18, 88–90
  profitability of, 9, 10, 11, 15, 17–21, 73, 88–90
  reluctance in, 8, 10, 11, 46–48, 51, 89
  tendency to offset open-market operations, 2, 9, 15, 16, 19, 88–90
  tradition against, 19, 20, 89
Bryan, William R., 48 n.
Burgess, W. Randolph, 8, 9, 23, 47 n.

Campbell, Colin D., 24 n.
Capital theory, application to analysis of deposit-expansion process, 49–58
Carr, Hobart C., 4 n., 24 n., 59
Clearings drains, 22, 24, 27, 28, 41–43, 48
Coleman, George, 73 n.
Crick, W. F., 24
Currie, Lauchlin, 3, 10, 11, 24, 25, 28, 29 n., 38 n., 48 n., 88

Deposit-expansion process, 10–14, 16, 30, 32–36, 58, 59, 90–93
Deposit-reserves ratio, 24–30, 34, 92, 93
Desired free-reserve ratio:
  of individual bank, 42–44
  of System, 44, 49–53
Desired reserve position
  concept of, 3, 4, 41–44
  determinants of, 45–53
Discount rate, 7, 9, 15, 19–21, 46, 47, 81, 82, 92
Discounting; see Borrowing by member banks
Distribution of deposits among banks
  influence on reserve positions, 10, 17, 23, 24, 48
  influence on reserve requirements, 13, 28, 37, 38, 93

Excess profits tax, influence on borrowing, 72, 73

Federal funds market, 43, 47, 48, 82
Free-reserve ratio
  accounting definitions, 33–36
  actual, 45
  behavior (1947–58), 37–39
  demand curve for, 50, 51
  desired, 43, 44, 46–49
  desired rate of change of, 50–53
Free-reserve theory, 1, 2, 23, 24, 66
Free reserves
  as indicator of monetary policy, 59–61, 93, 94
  as objective for open-market operations, 57–59, 66, 83, 86–92
Freutel, Guy S., 2 n.
Friedman, Milton, 3, 4 n., 24 n., 29, 45 n., 49

Hardy, Charles O., 3, 14–16, 88
Harris, Seymour, 16–18, 88
Hart, Albert G., 34 n.
Horwich, George, 25, 26–27, 38 n., 82

Interbank deposits, 43, 44
Interbank lending, 43, 44, 47, 48, 82
Interest rates, determination of, 60, 61, 88, 89

Kareken, John H., 30 n.
Keynes, John Maynard, 18, 19, 25

Liquidity trap, 29, 30

McDonald, Stephen L., 25 n.
McKinney, George W., 47 n.
Melton, W. G., 43 n.
Meltzer, Allan H., 3, 25, 27, 28 n., 43 n., 48
Monetary policy objectives, 1, 2, 92
Money supply, determinants of, 6, 10–14, 16, 21, 22, 32–36, 90–93
Morrison, George R., 30, 47, 48
Multiple-expansion coefficient, 24–30, 34

117

Open-market operations, 7–9, 14–18, 34–
36, 57–59, 83–85, 87, 88, 90–93
Orr, Daniel, 43 n.

Polak, J. J., 3, 21, 22, 69
Polakoff, Murray E., 21 n., 51 n., 89

Regulation A, 46, 47, 51, 73, 80–82, 89
Reluctance to borrow, 8, 10, 11, 46–48,
51, 89
Required reserves ratio
accounting definition 33
behavior (1947–58), 37–39
Reserve factor accounting, 17, 34–36
Reserve position doctrine
criticism of, 14–19
free reserves variant, 23, 24
modified, 92, 93
origin of, 7–10
Reserve requirements, 13, 25, 26, 28, 29,
33, 34, 36–41, 93
Reserves
effective, 26, 27
excess, 9, 18, 27–30
legal, 27, 28
net, 23–24
precautionary, 27, 43
required, 13
unborrowed, 35–41, 53–56
Reserves-deposits ratio, 24–30
Response lags, 15, 16, 26–29, 51, 62, 82–
86, 88

Riefler, Winfield W., 3, 6, 8–10, 14, 15,
17, 23, 24 n., 27 n., 88–89
Roosa, Robert V., 24 n., 47 n., 81 n.

Seasonality
influence on desired reserve position,
48, 49
tests for, 74–77
Secondary equilibrium position, definition, 55, 56
Simmons, Edward C., 28, 29 n., 38 n.,
46, 47 n.
Smith, Warren L., 21 n.
Sprinkel, Beryl W., 88 n.
Stock-flow analysis, 49–58

Tinbergen, Jan, 3, 11–14, 38 n., 68, 69 n.,
88–89
Tolley, George, 29 n., 38 n.
Treasury-Federal Reserve accord, influ-
ence on free-reserve ratio, 71, 72
Turner, Robert C., 3, 19–21, 82

Vault cash, 17, 34, 35, 44, 45

Walker, Charls E., 47 n.
Warburton, Clark, 3, 38 n.
White, William H., 3, 21, 22, 69
Whittlesey, Charles R., 47 n., 81 n.

Young, Ralph A., 4 n., 24 n.